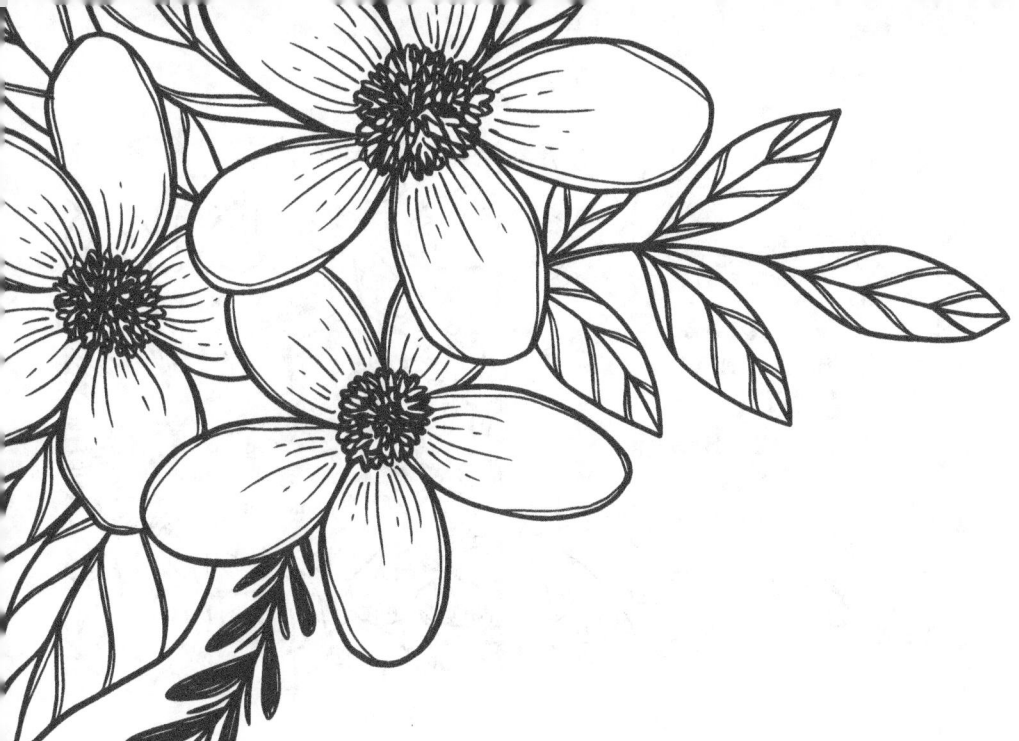

This Bible Verse

COLORING BOOK BELONGS TO

_____

_____

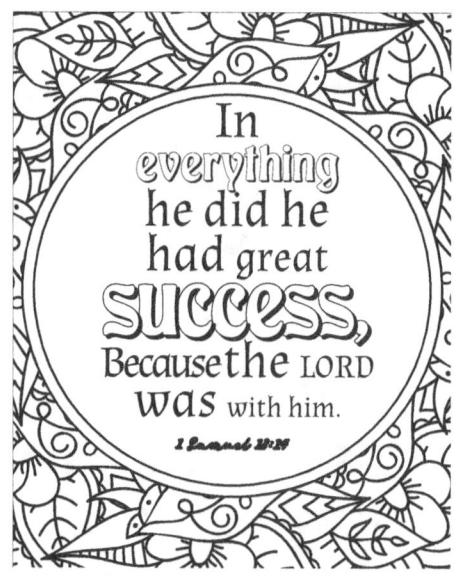

In everything he did he had great **SUCCESS**, Because the LORD was with him.

1 Samuel 18:14

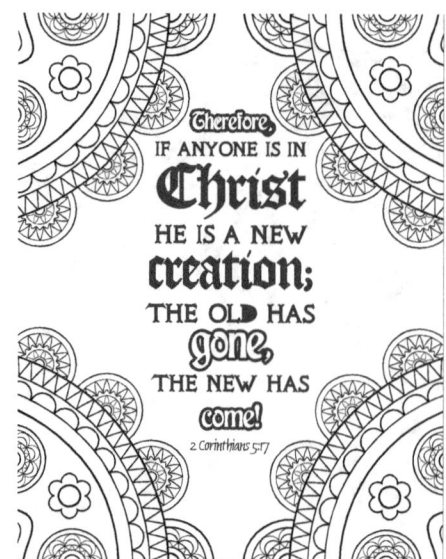

Therefore, IF ANYONE IS IN **Christ** HE IS A NEW **creation**; THE OLD HAS **gone**, THE NEW HAS **come!**

2 Corinthians 5:17

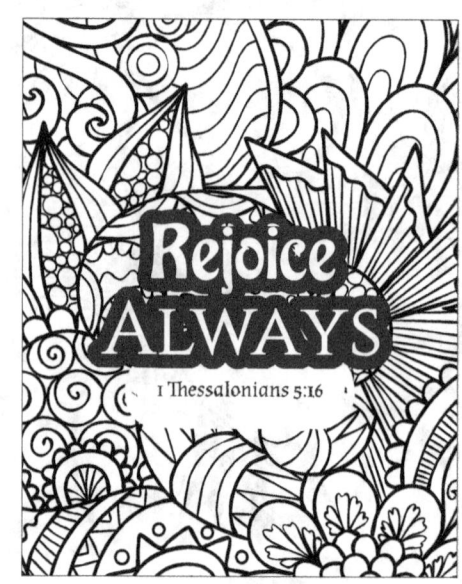

Rejoice ALWAYS

1 Thessalonians 5:16

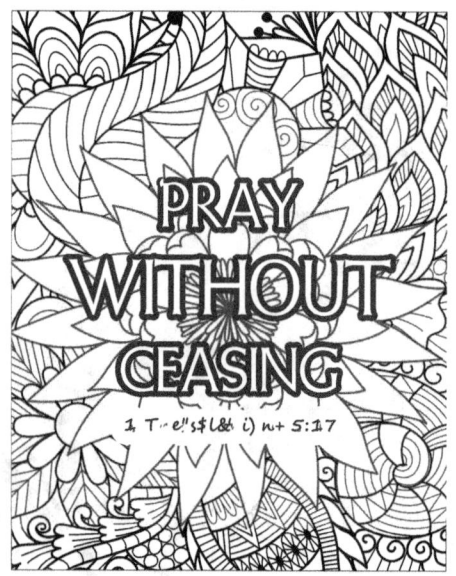

PRAY WITHOUT CEASING

1 Thessalonians 5:17

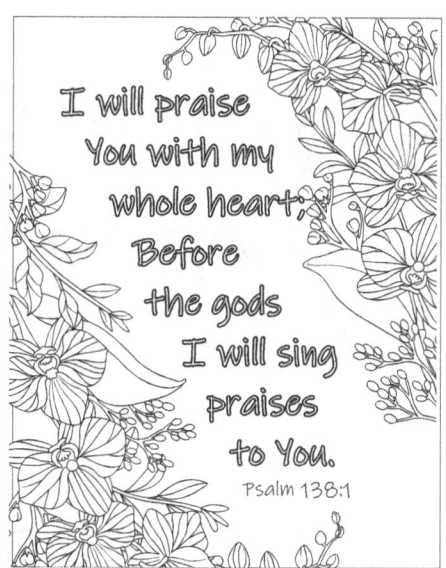

I will praise You with my whole heart; Before the gods I will sing praises to You.

Psalm 138:1

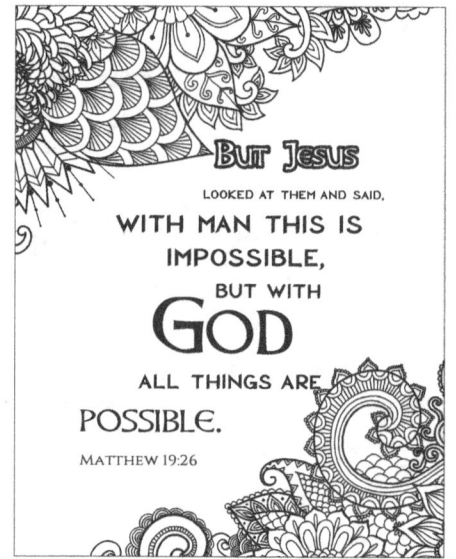

But Jesus LOOKED AT THEM AND SAID, WITH MAN THIS IS IMPOSSIBLE, BUT WITH **GOD** ALL THINGS ARE POSSIBLE.

MATTHEW 19:26

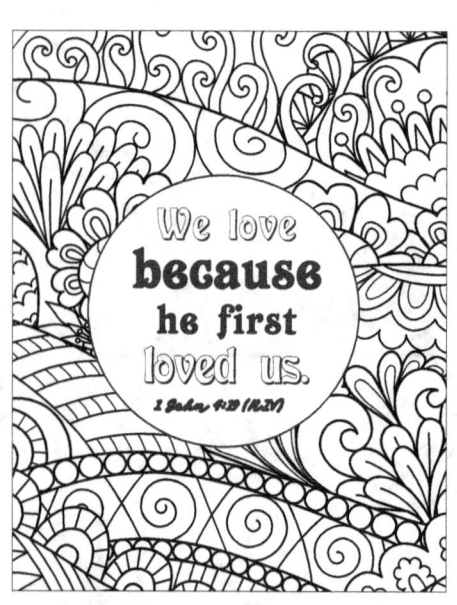

We love **because** he first loved us.

1 John 4:19 (NLT)

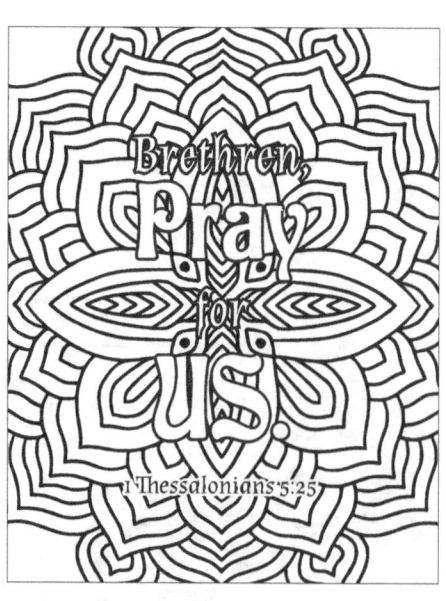

Brethren, Pray for us.

1 Thessalonians 5:25

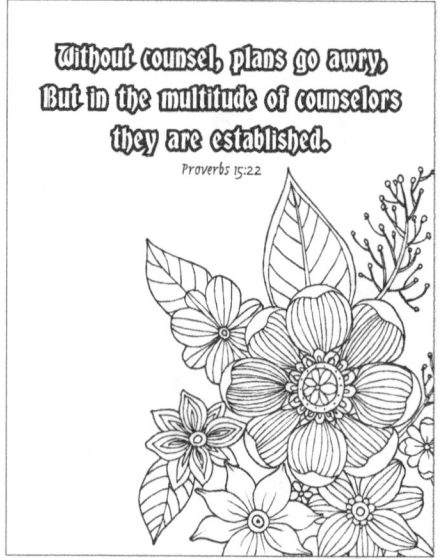

Without counsel, plans go awry, But in the multitude of counselors they are established.

Proverbs 15:22

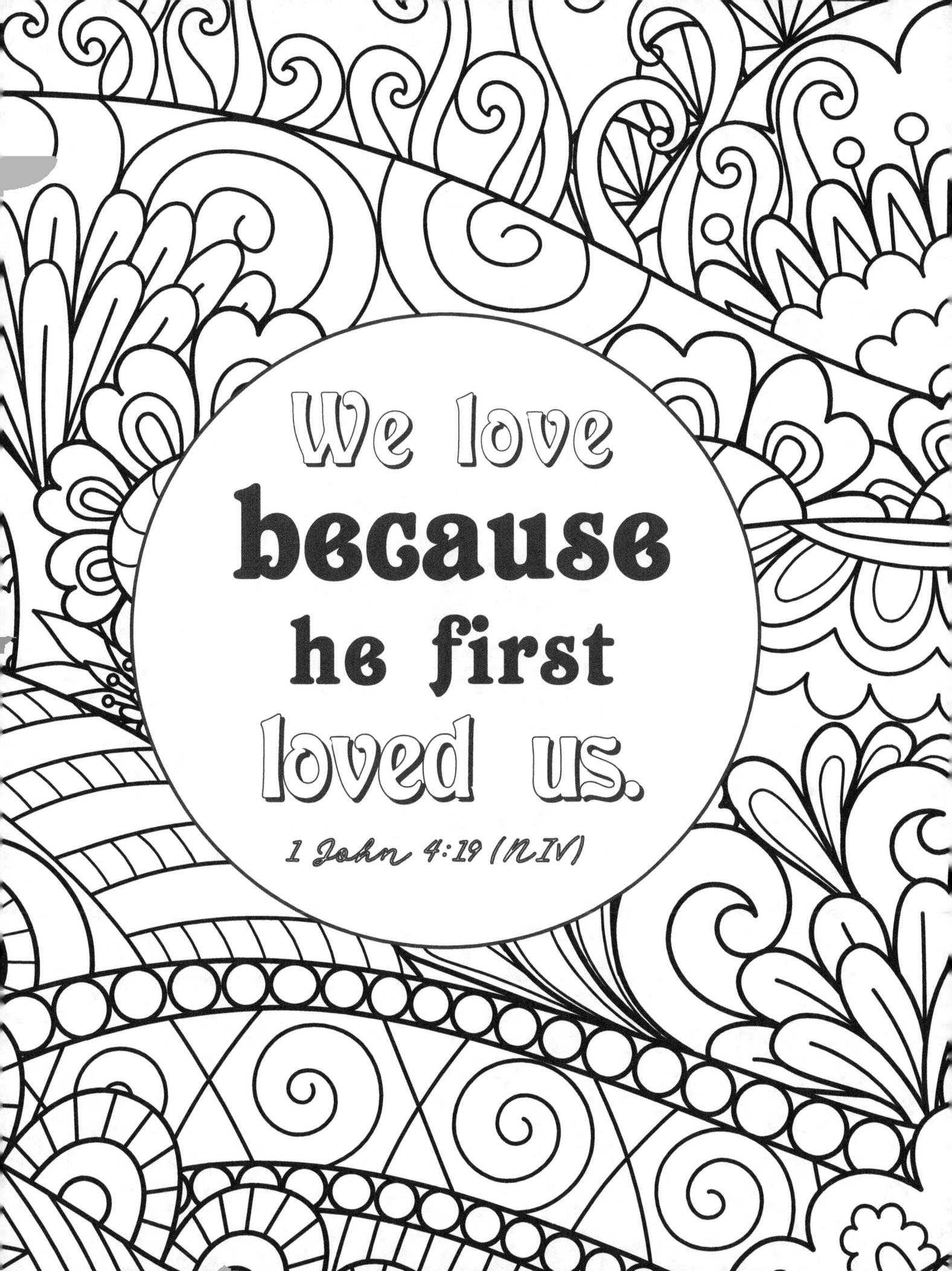

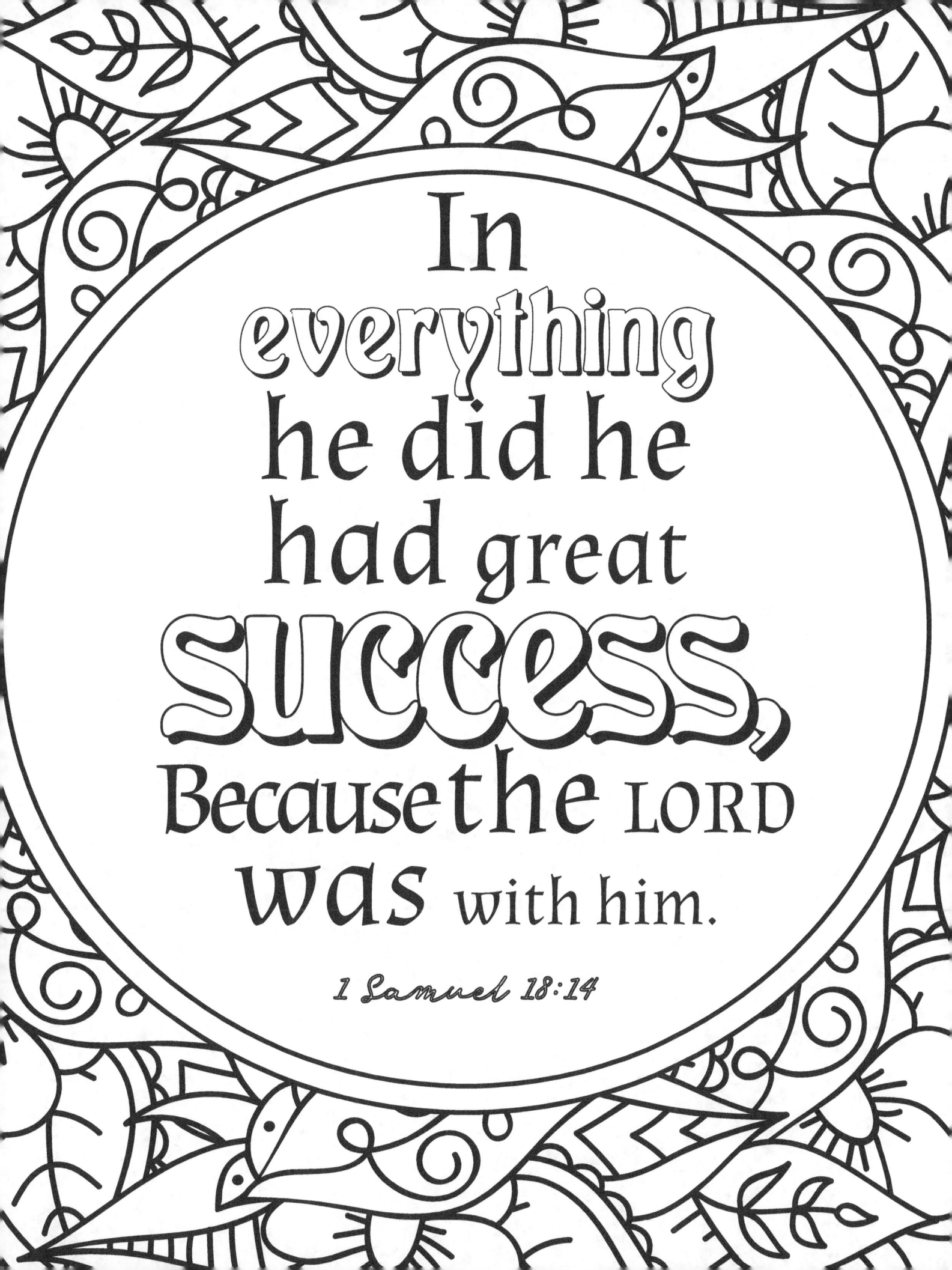

In everything he did he had great SUCCESS, Because the LORD was with him.

1 Samuel 18:14

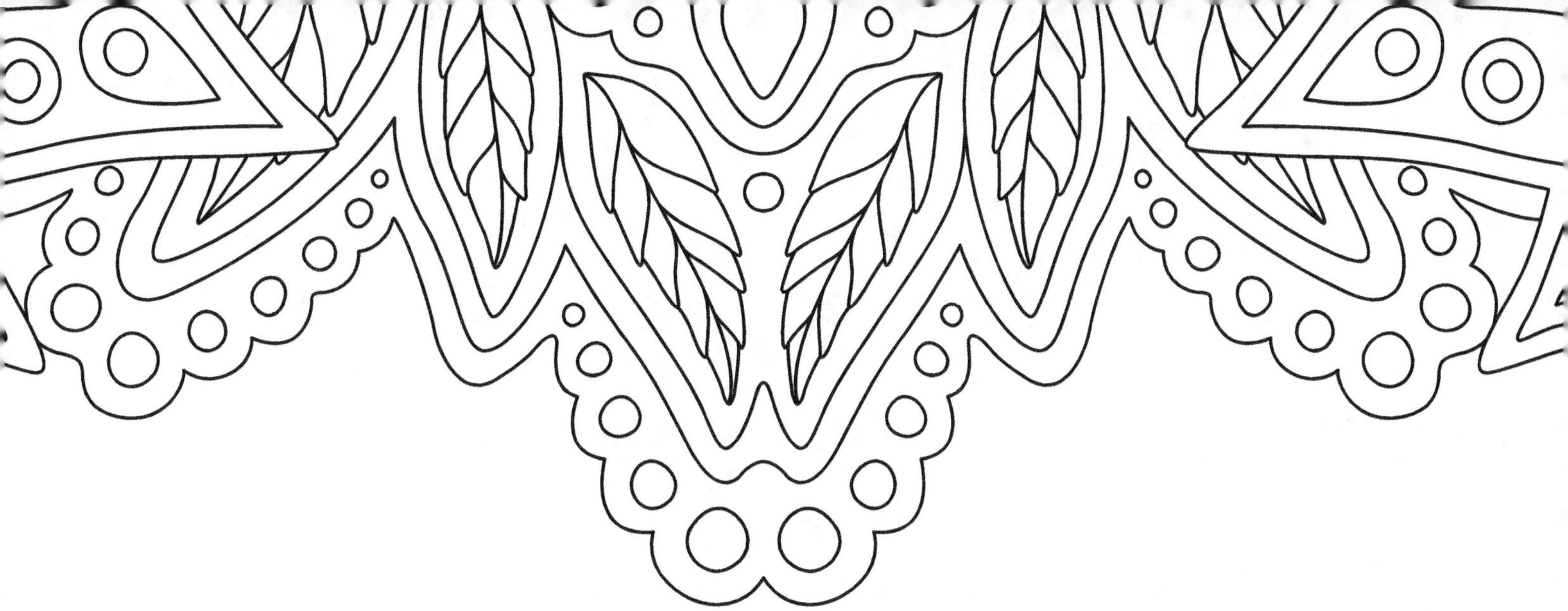

For this is the love of God, that we keep His COMMANDMENTS. And His COMMANDMENTS are not BURDENSOME.

1 John 5:3

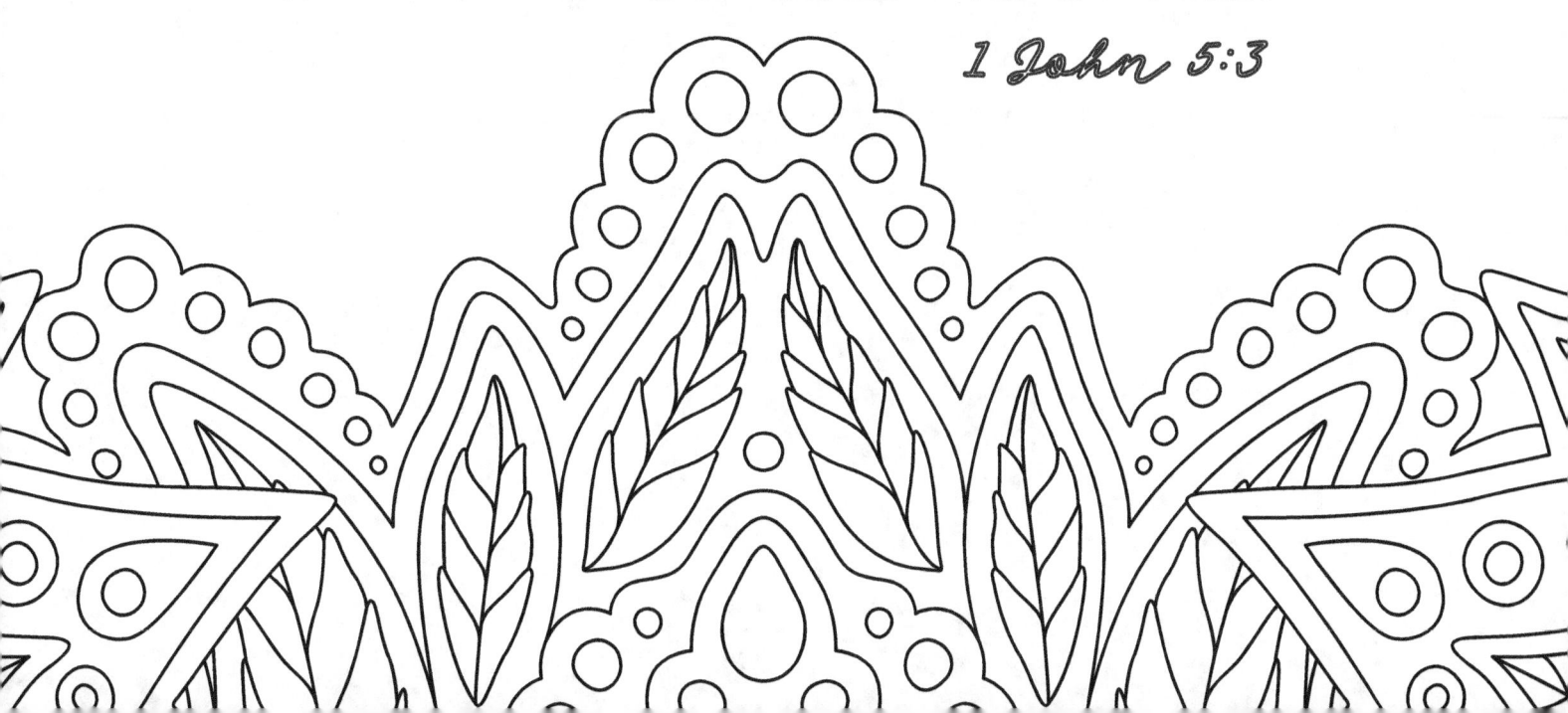

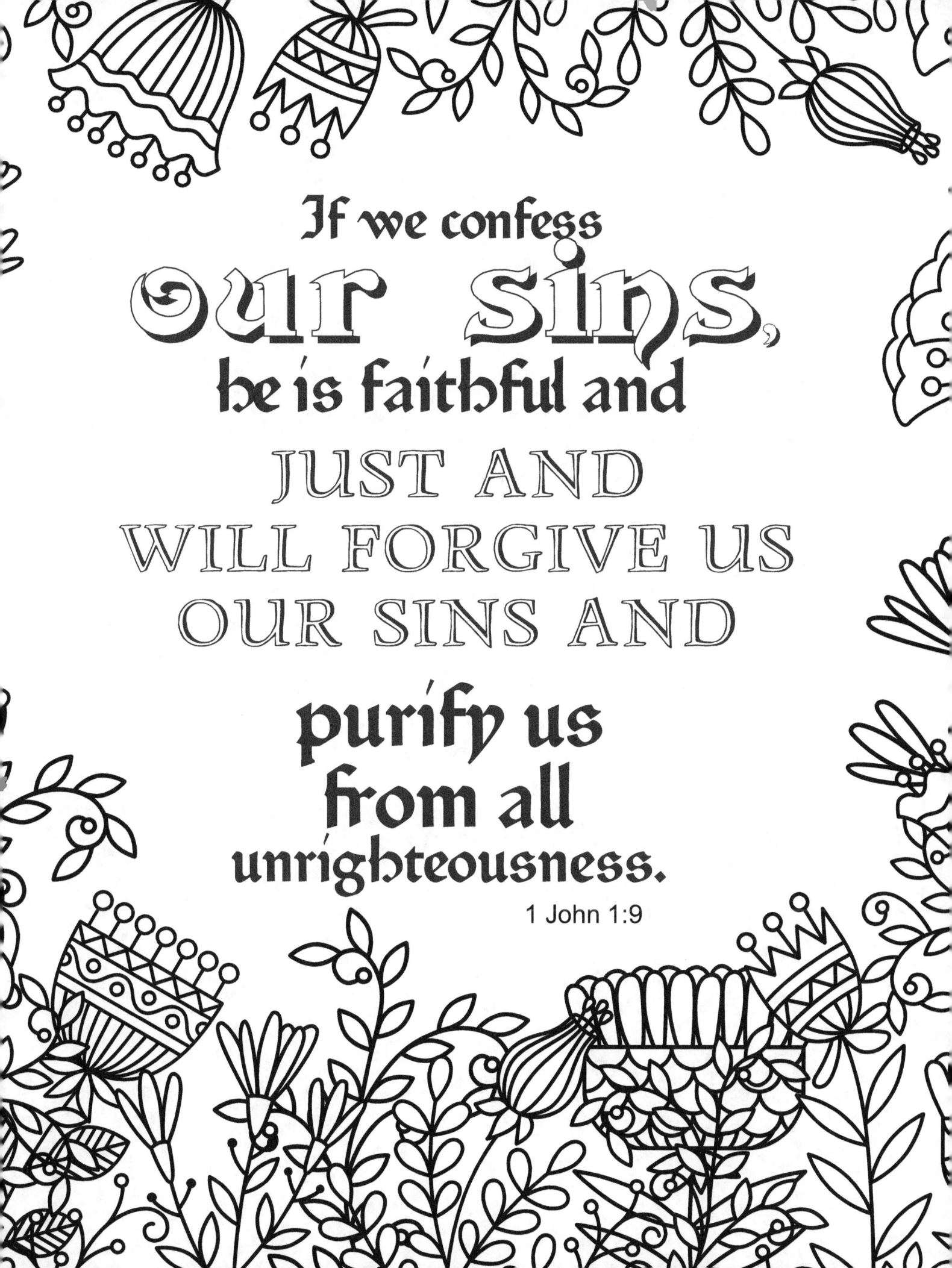

If we confess **Our sins,** he is faithful and JUST AND WILL FORGIVE US OUR SINS AND purify us from all unrighteousness.

1 John 1:9

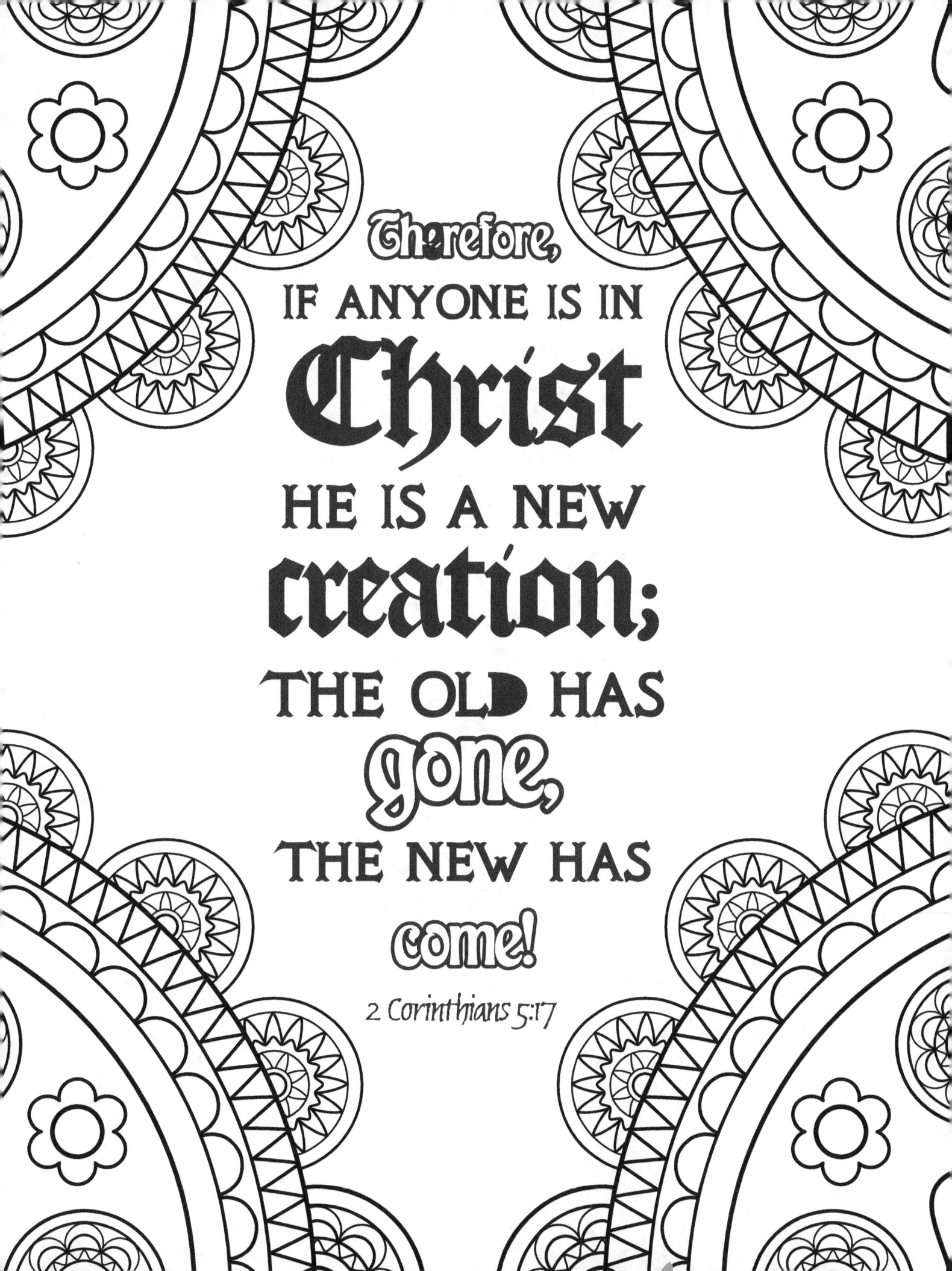

Therefore, IF ANYONE IS IN Christ HE IS A NEW creation; THE OLD HAS gone, THE NEW HAS come!

2 Corinthians 5:17

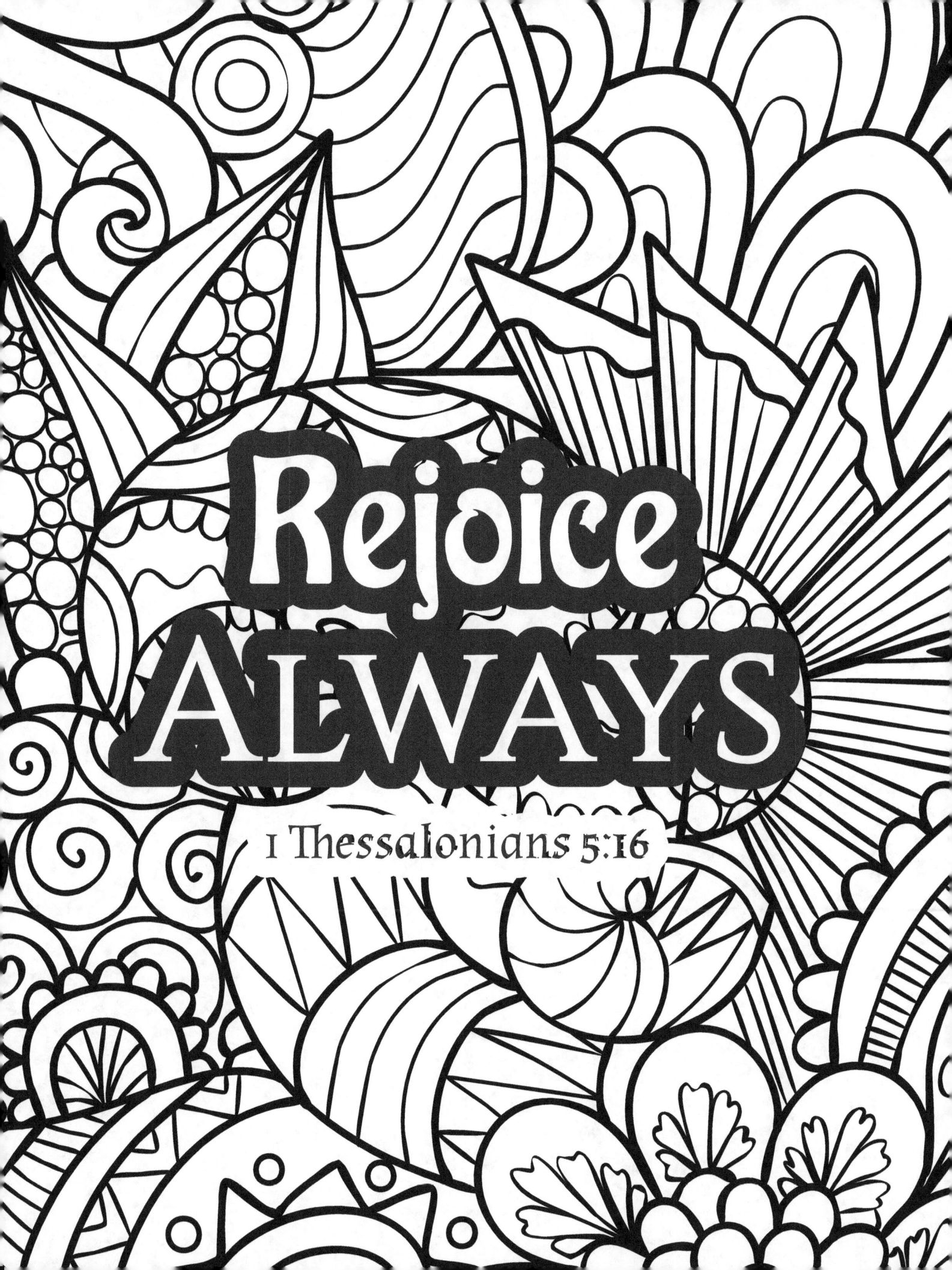

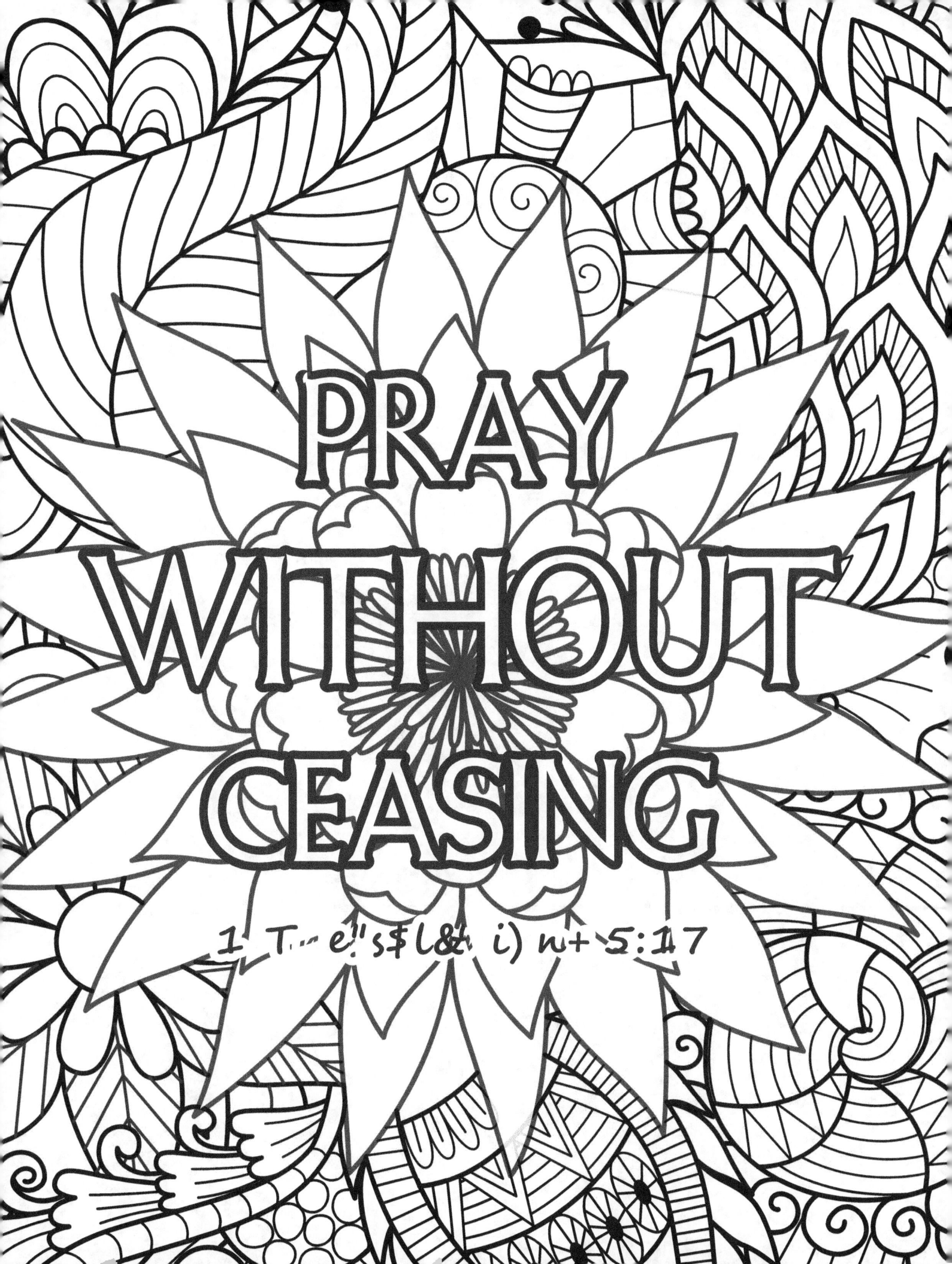

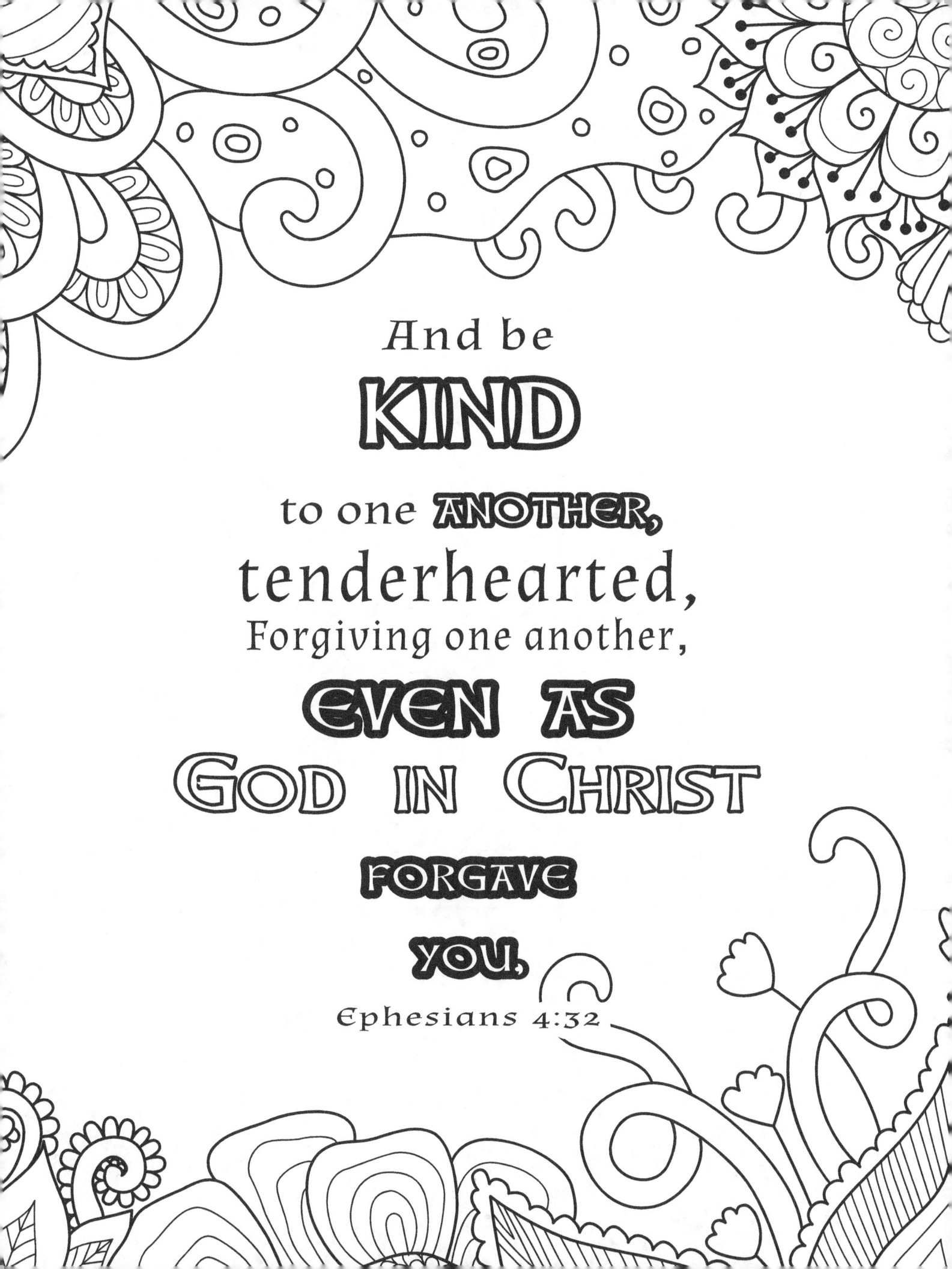

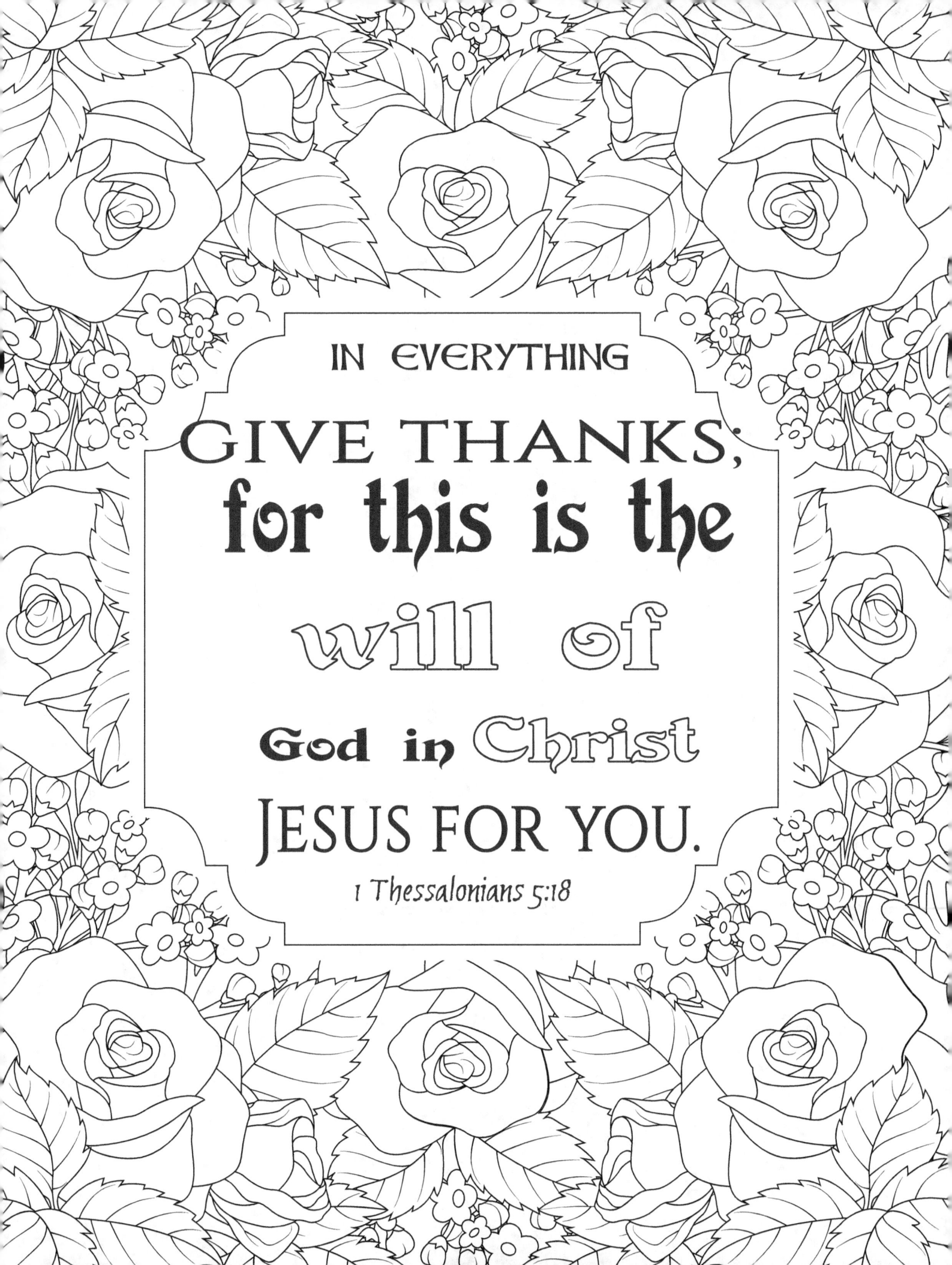

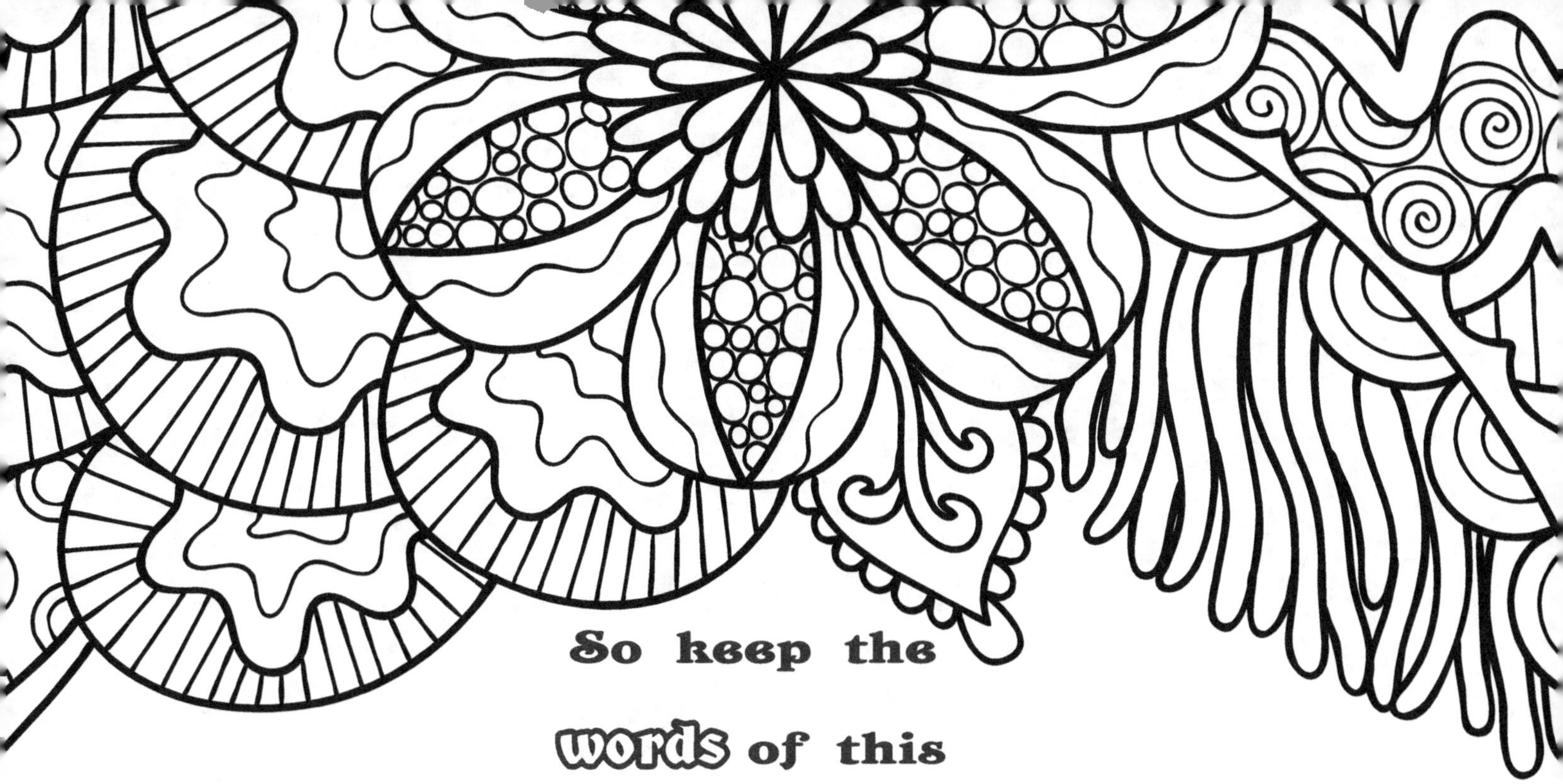

So keep the
words of this
covenant
to do them, that you may
prosper
in all that
you do.

Deuteronomy 29:9

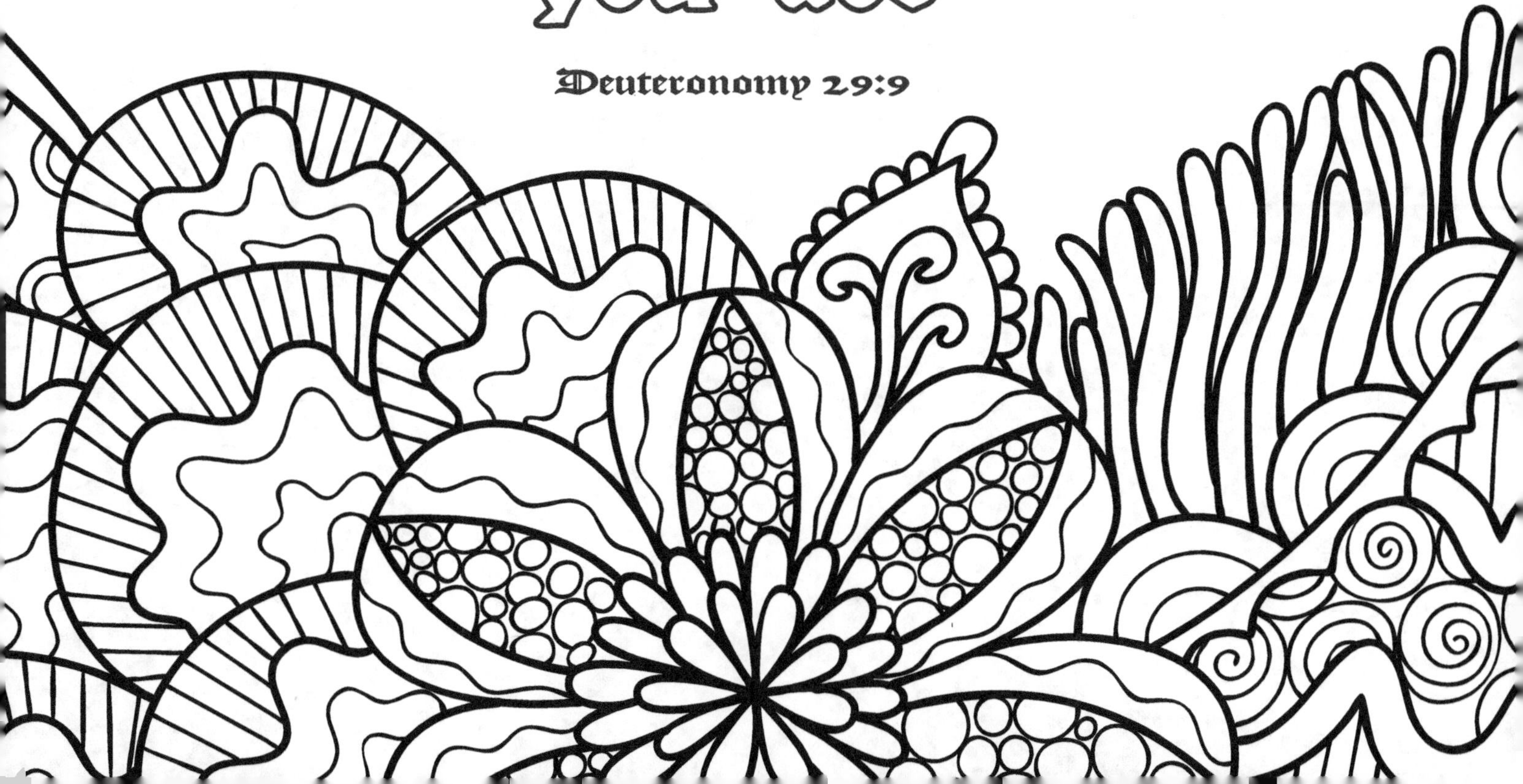

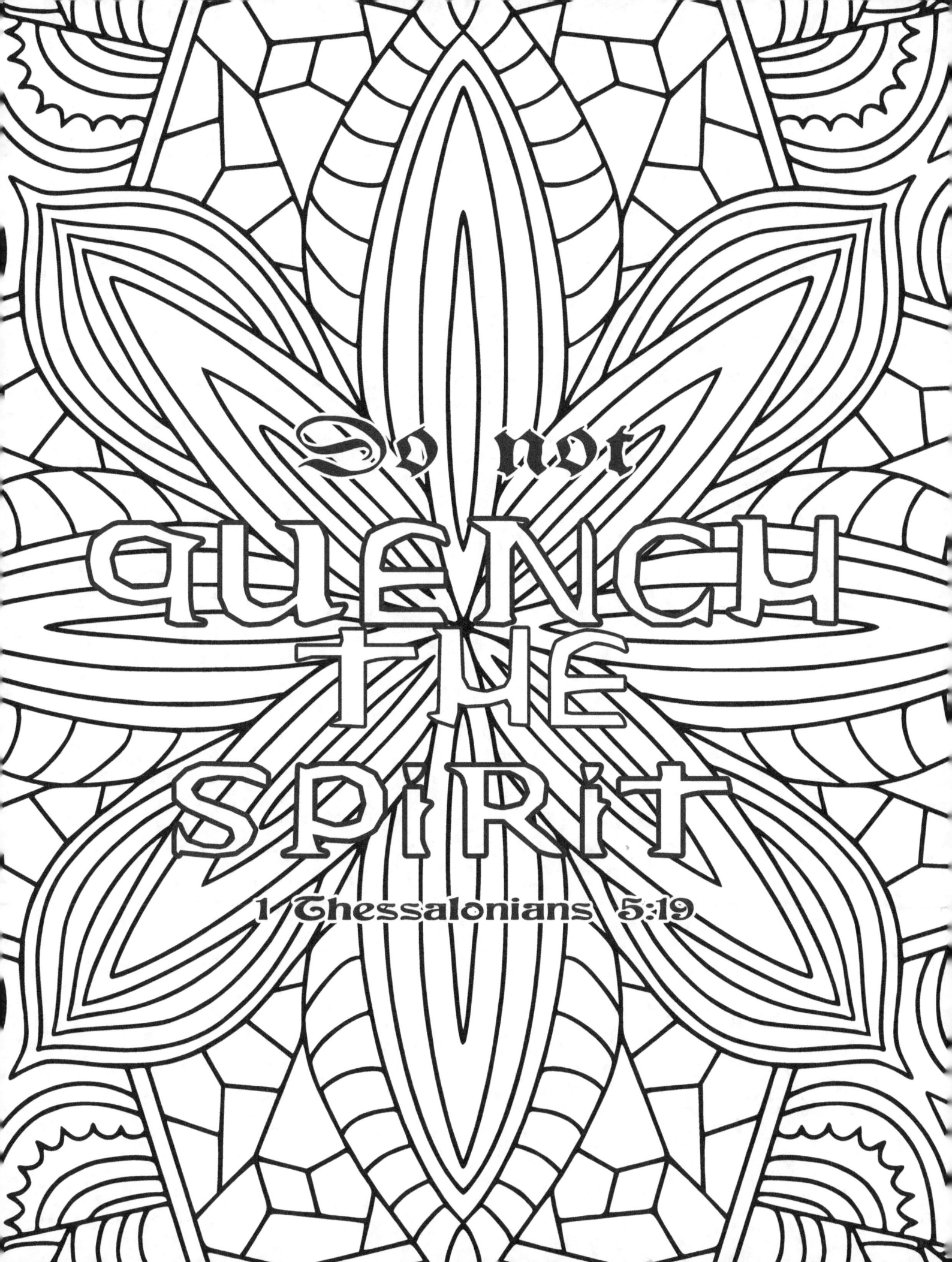

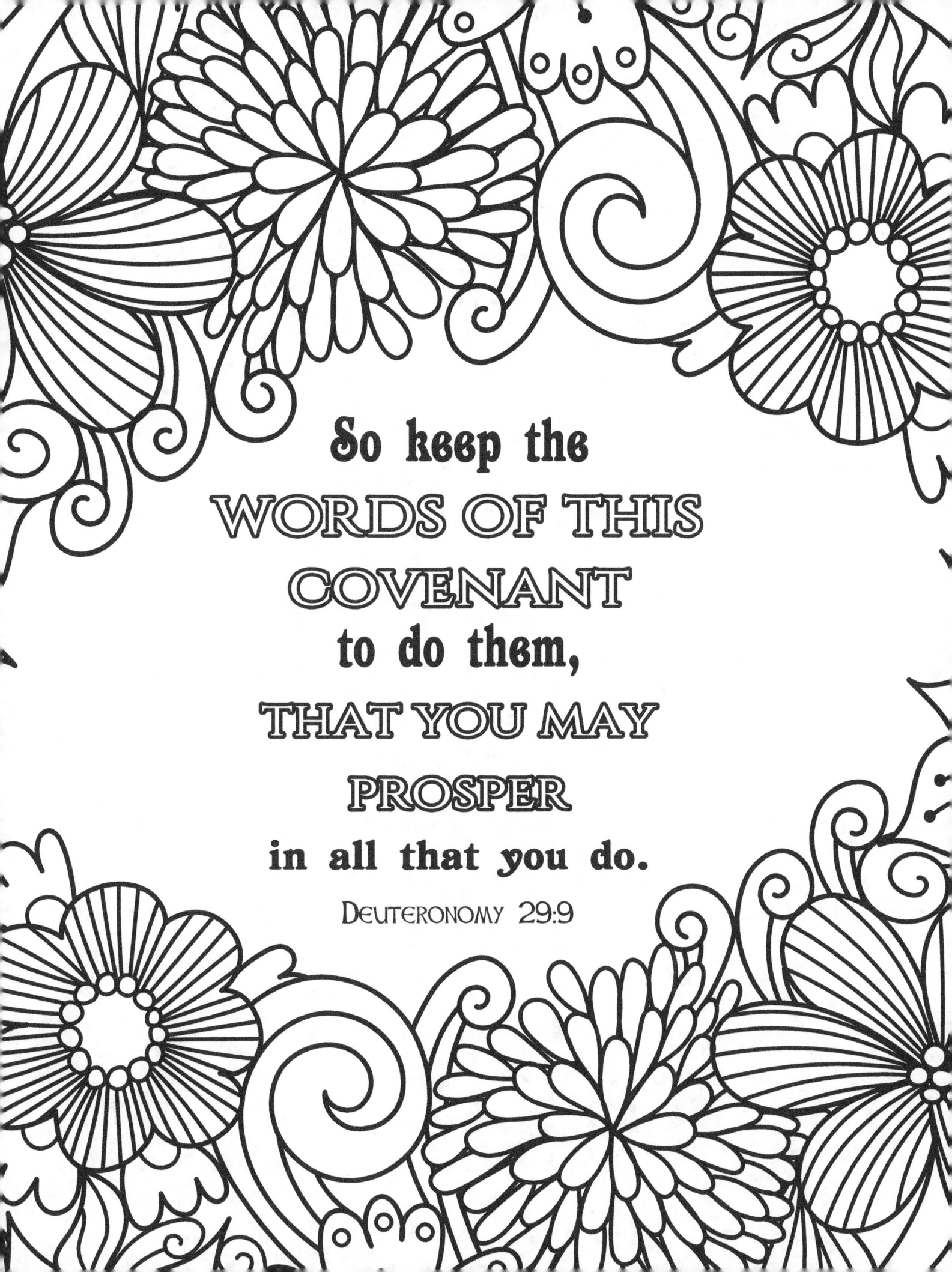

So keep the
WORDS OF THIS
COVENANT
to do them,
THAT YOU MAY
PROSPER
in all that you do.
Deuteronomy 29:9

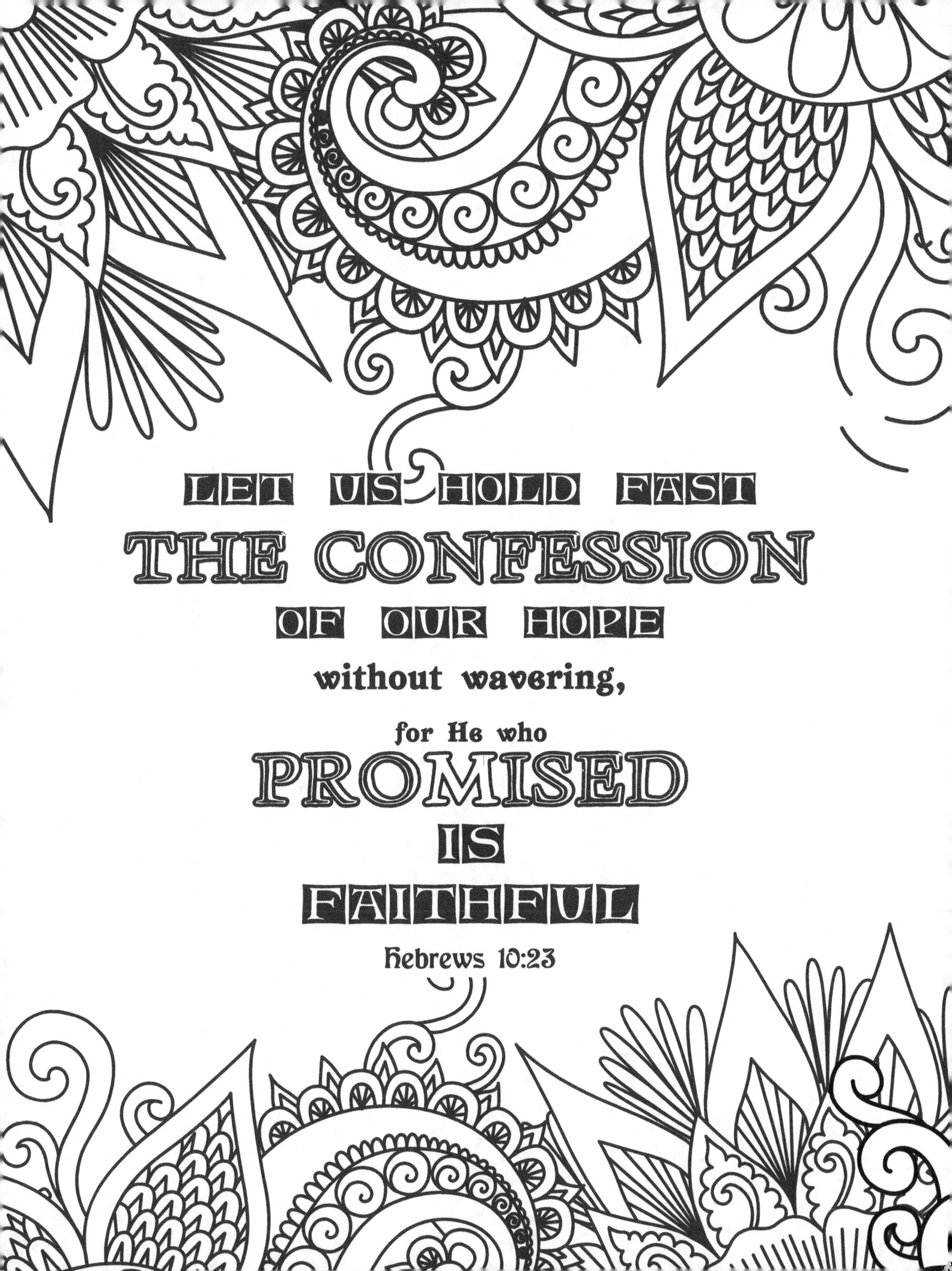

LET US HOLD FAST
THE CONFESSION
OF OUR HOPE
without wavering,
for He who
PROMISED
IS
FAITHFUL
Hebrews 10:23

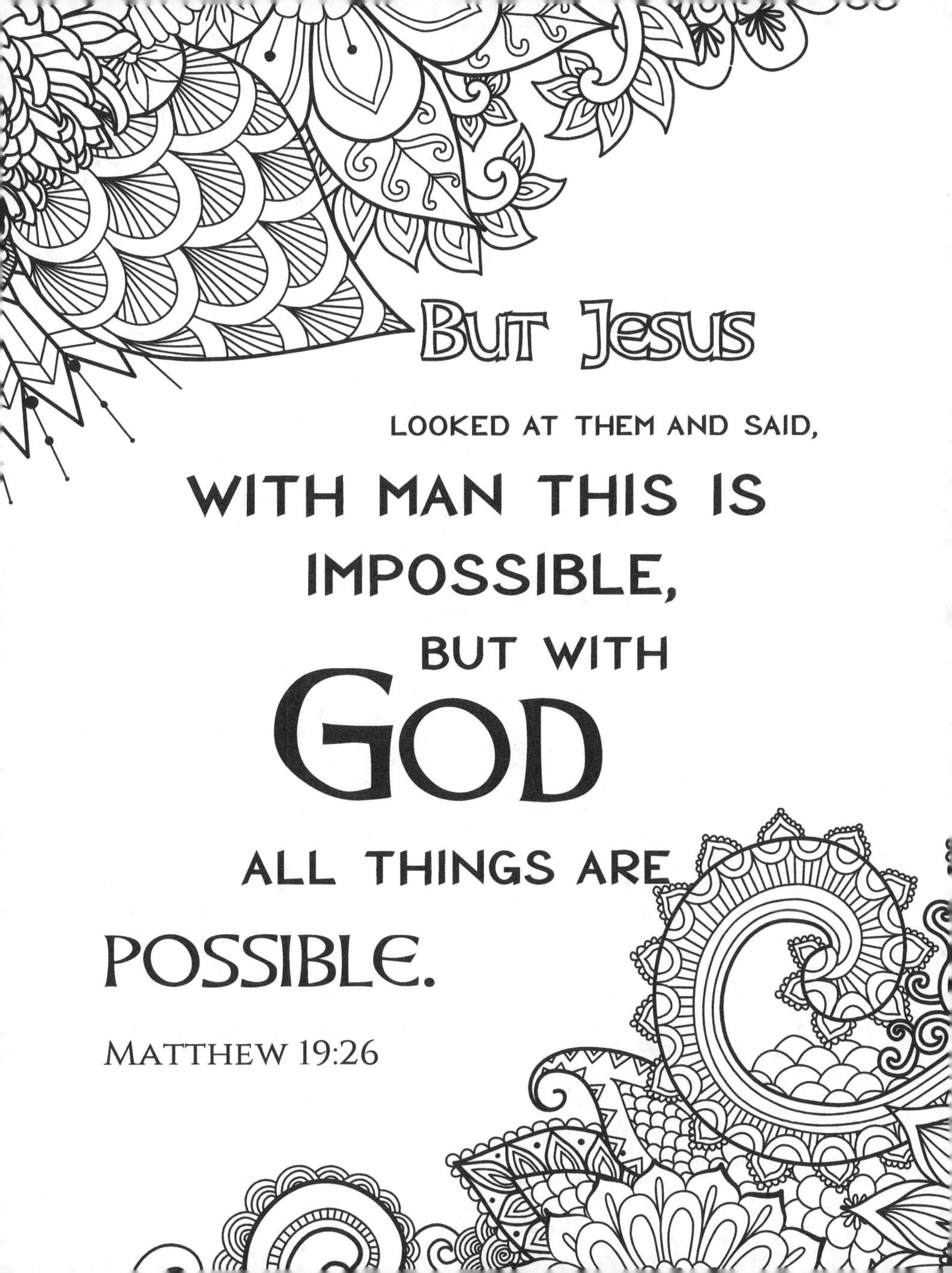

But Jesus

LOOKED AT THEM AND SAID,

WITH MAN THIS IS IMPOSSIBLE, BUT WITH GOD ALL THINGS ARE POSSIBLE.

MATTHEW 19:26

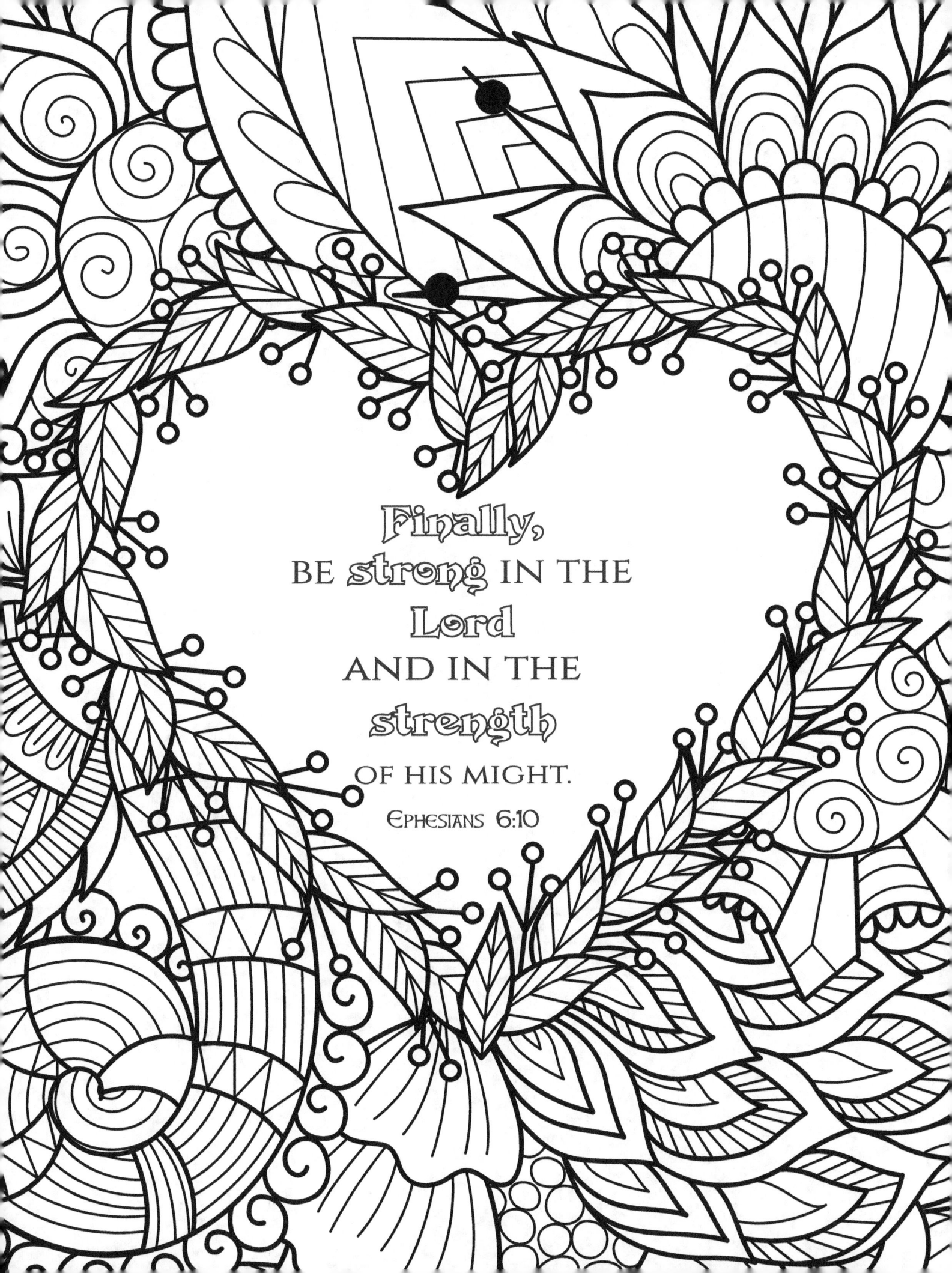

Finally,
BE strong IN THE
Lord
AND IN THE
strength
OF HIS MIGHT.
Ephesians 6:10

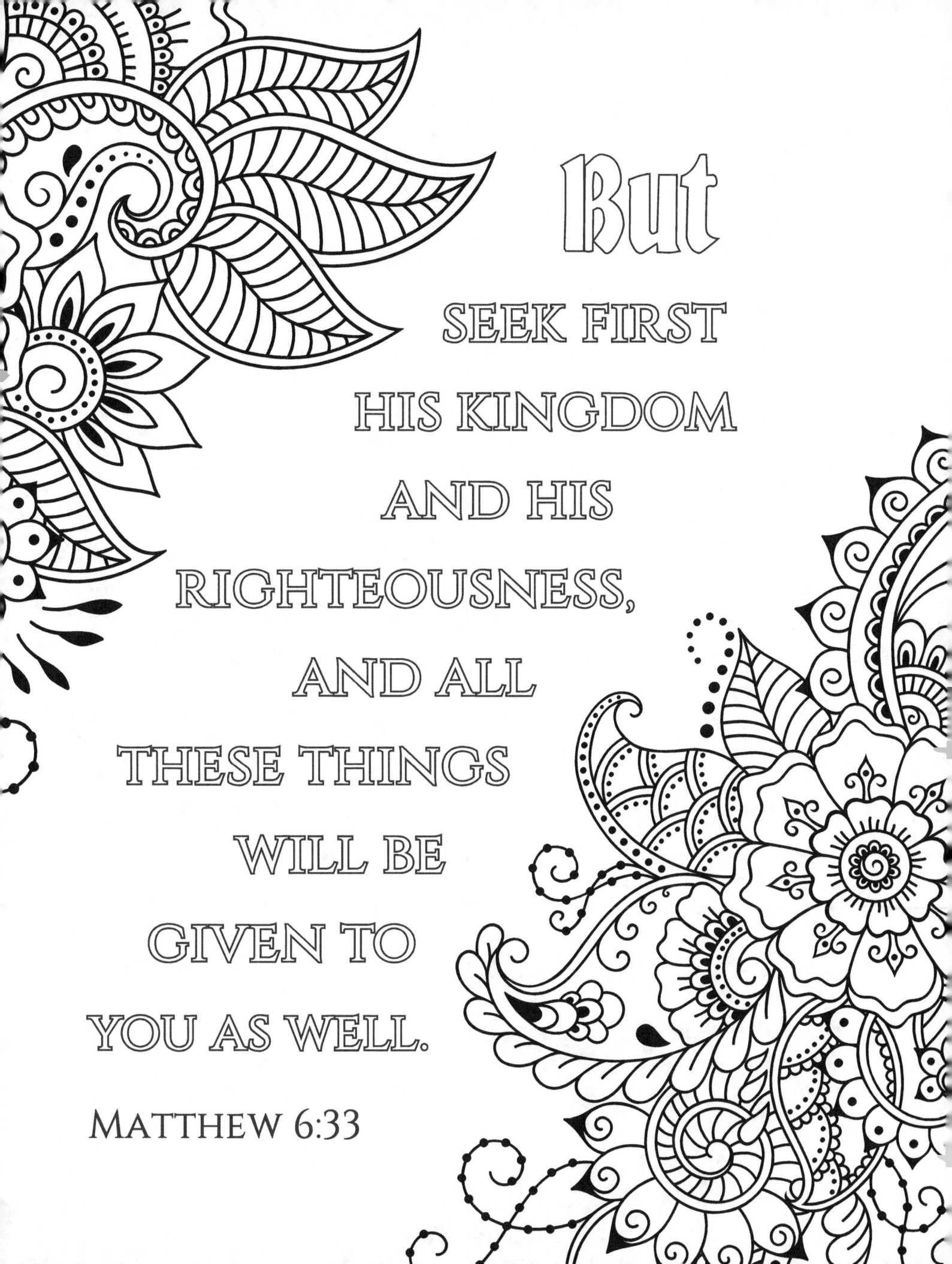

But

SEEK FIRST
HIS KINGDOM
AND HIS
RIGHTEOUSNESS,
AND ALL
THESE THINGS
WILL BE
GIVEN TO
YOU AS WELL.

MATTHEW 6:33

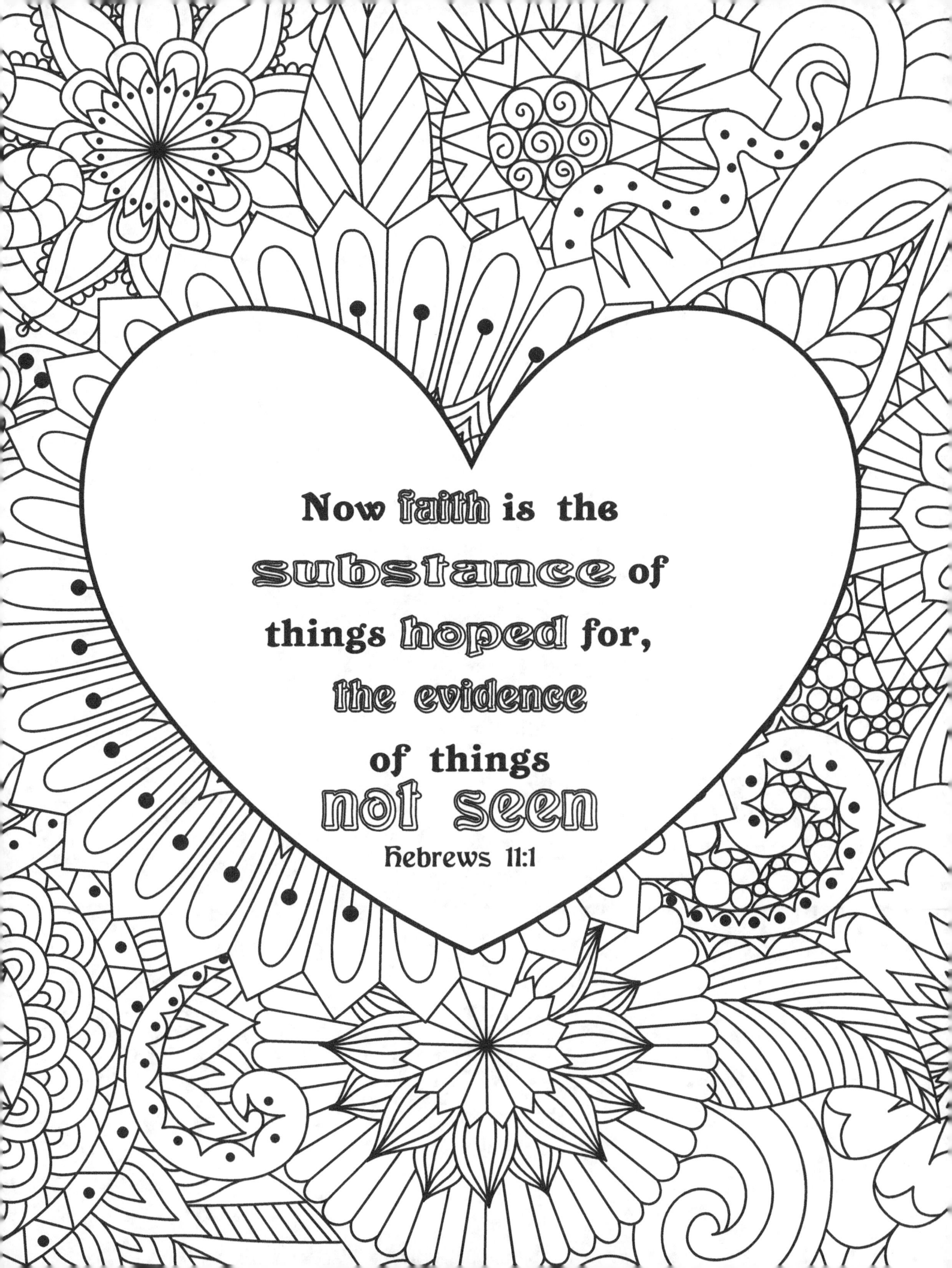

Now faith is the substance of things hoped for, the evidence of things not seen

Hebrews 11:1

Brethren, Pray for us.

1 Thessalonians 5:25

Without counsel, plans go awry, But in the multitude of counselors they are established.

Proverbs 15:22

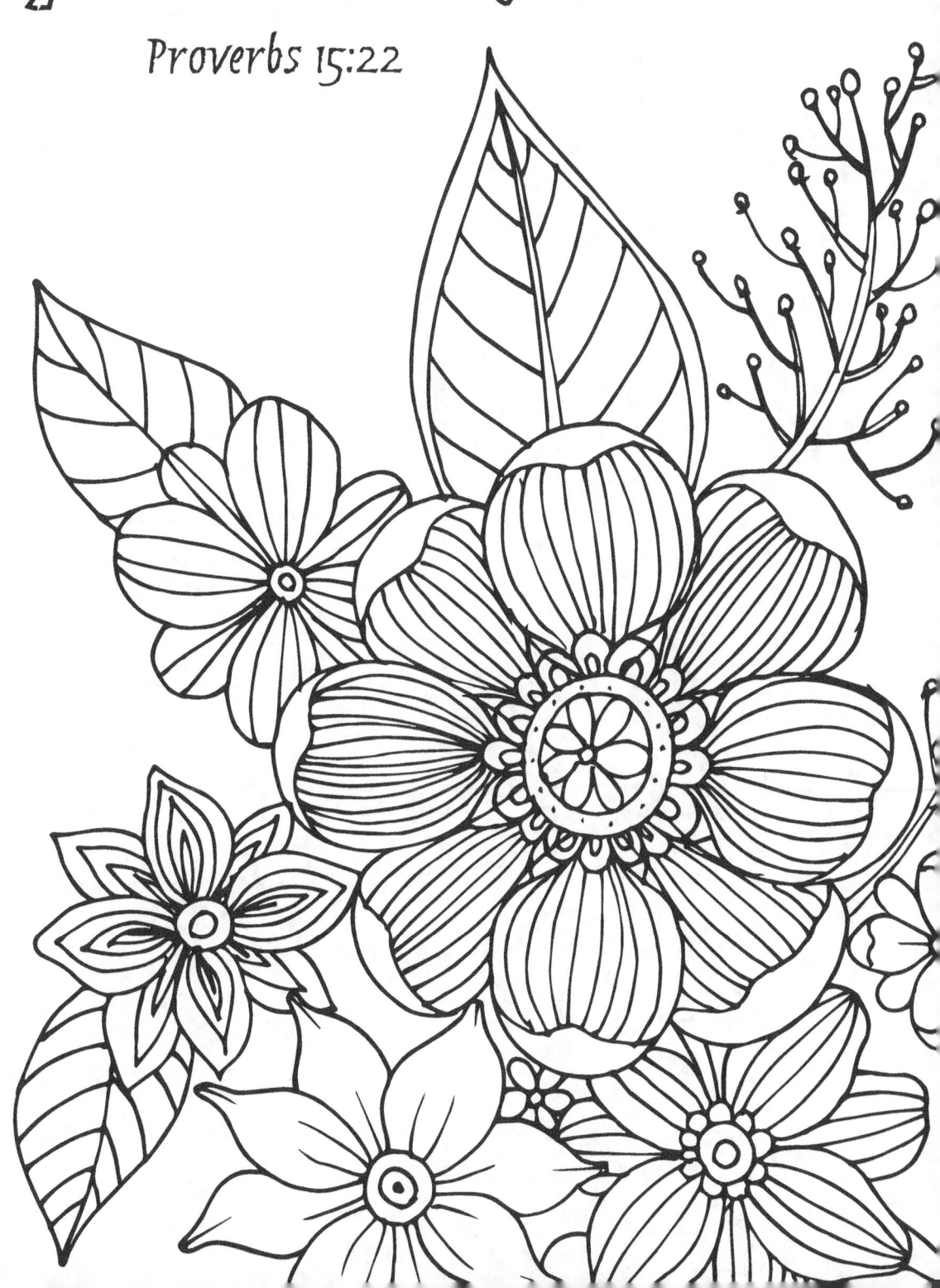

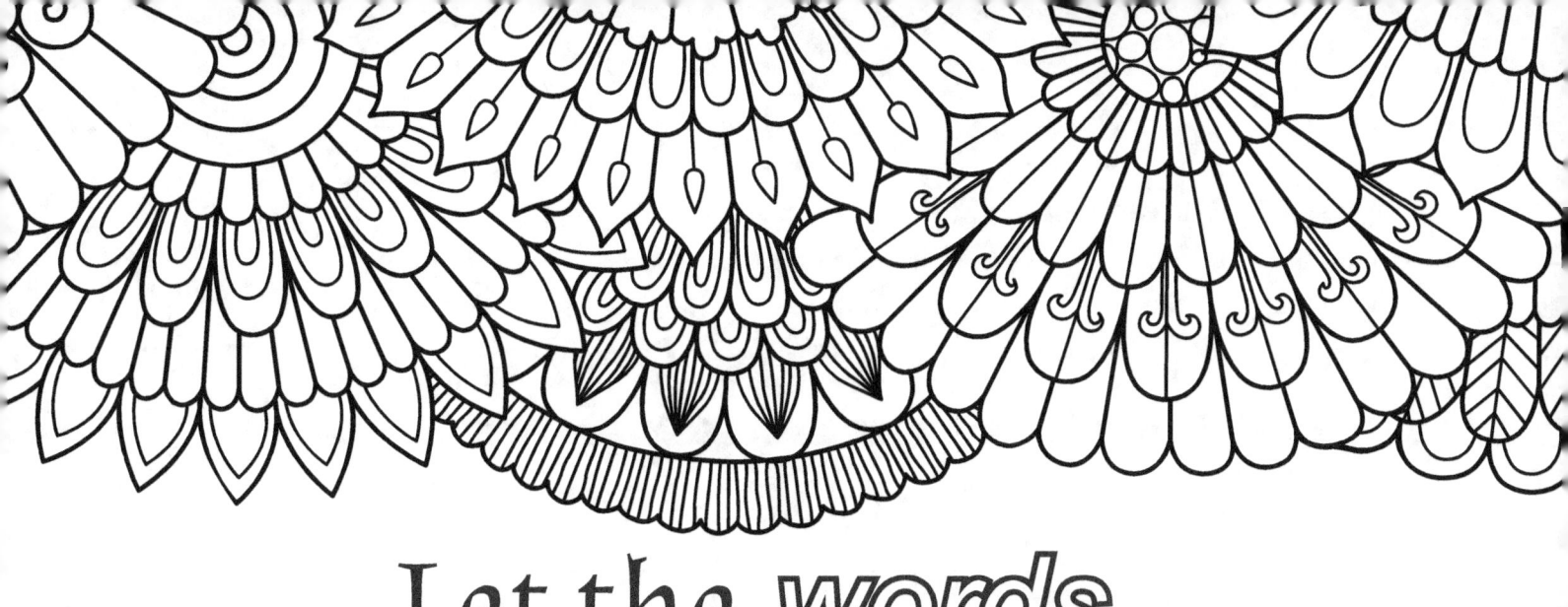

Let the *words*
of my mouth
and the *meditation*
of my heart
Be *acceptable*
in **Your Sight**

Psalm 19:14

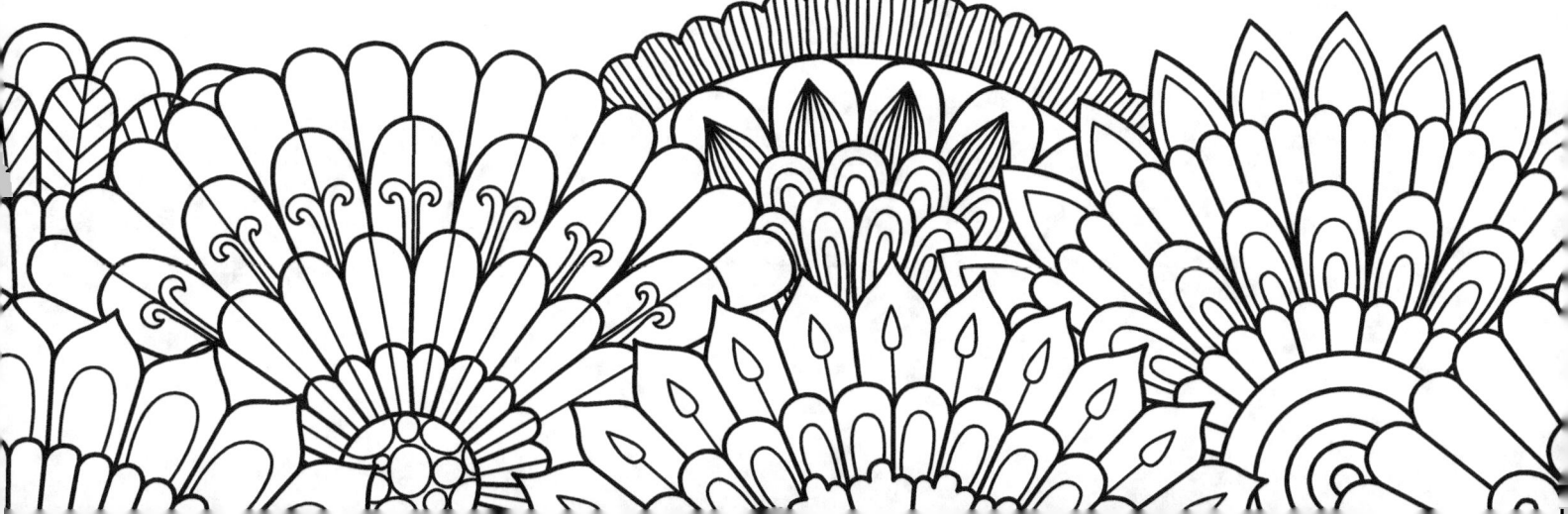

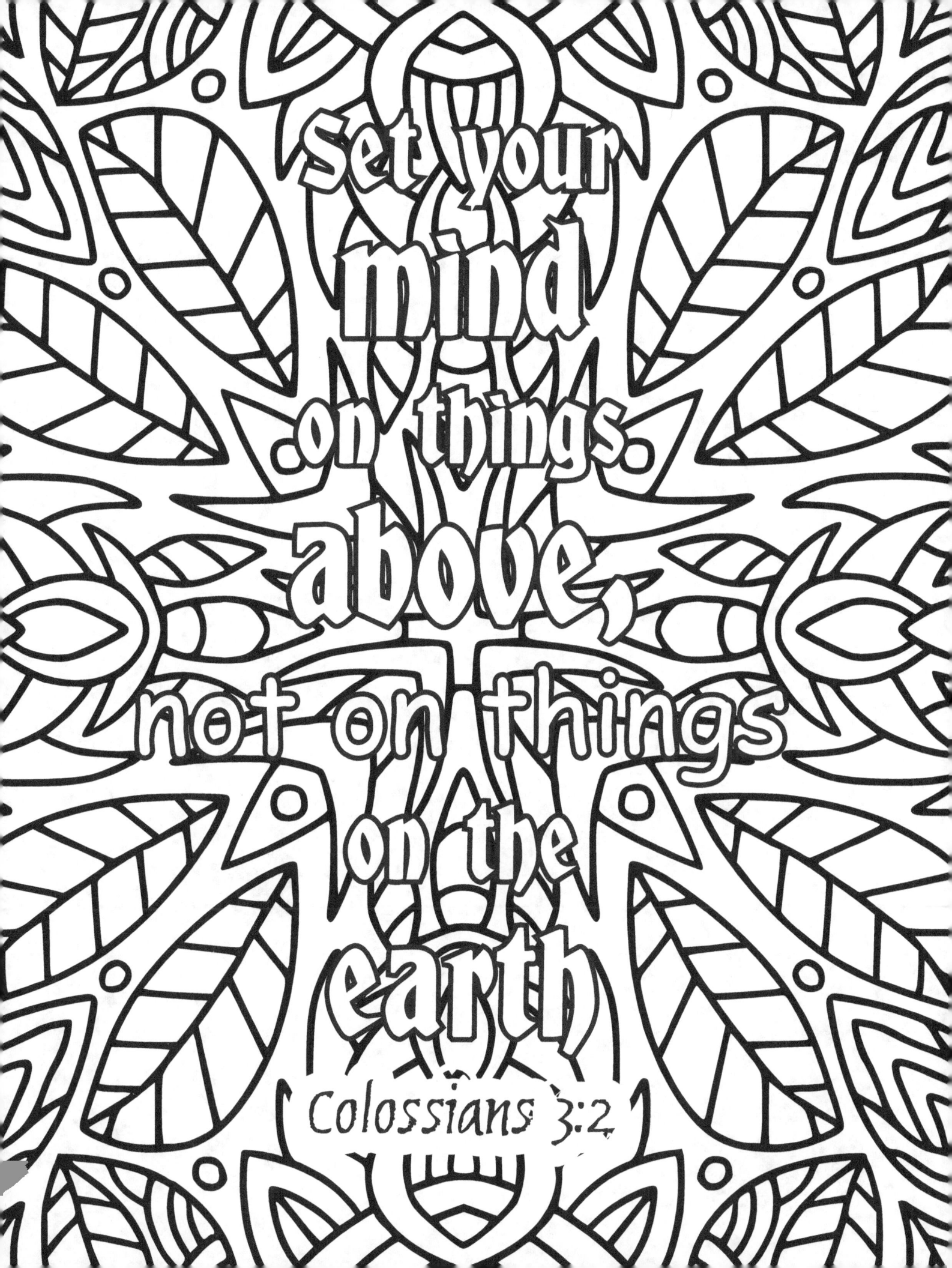

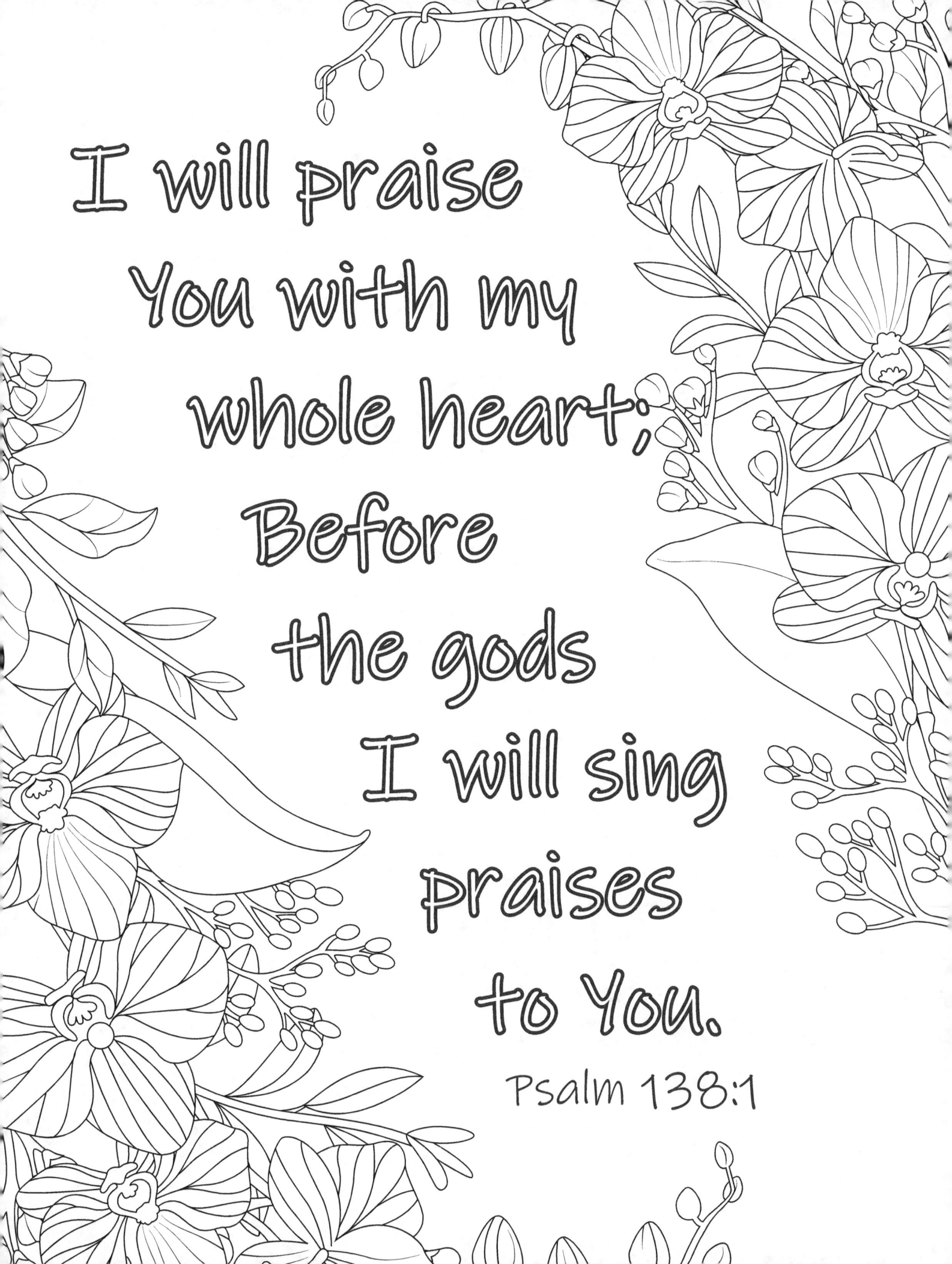

I will praise You with my whole heart; Before the gods I will sing praises to You.

Psalm 138:1

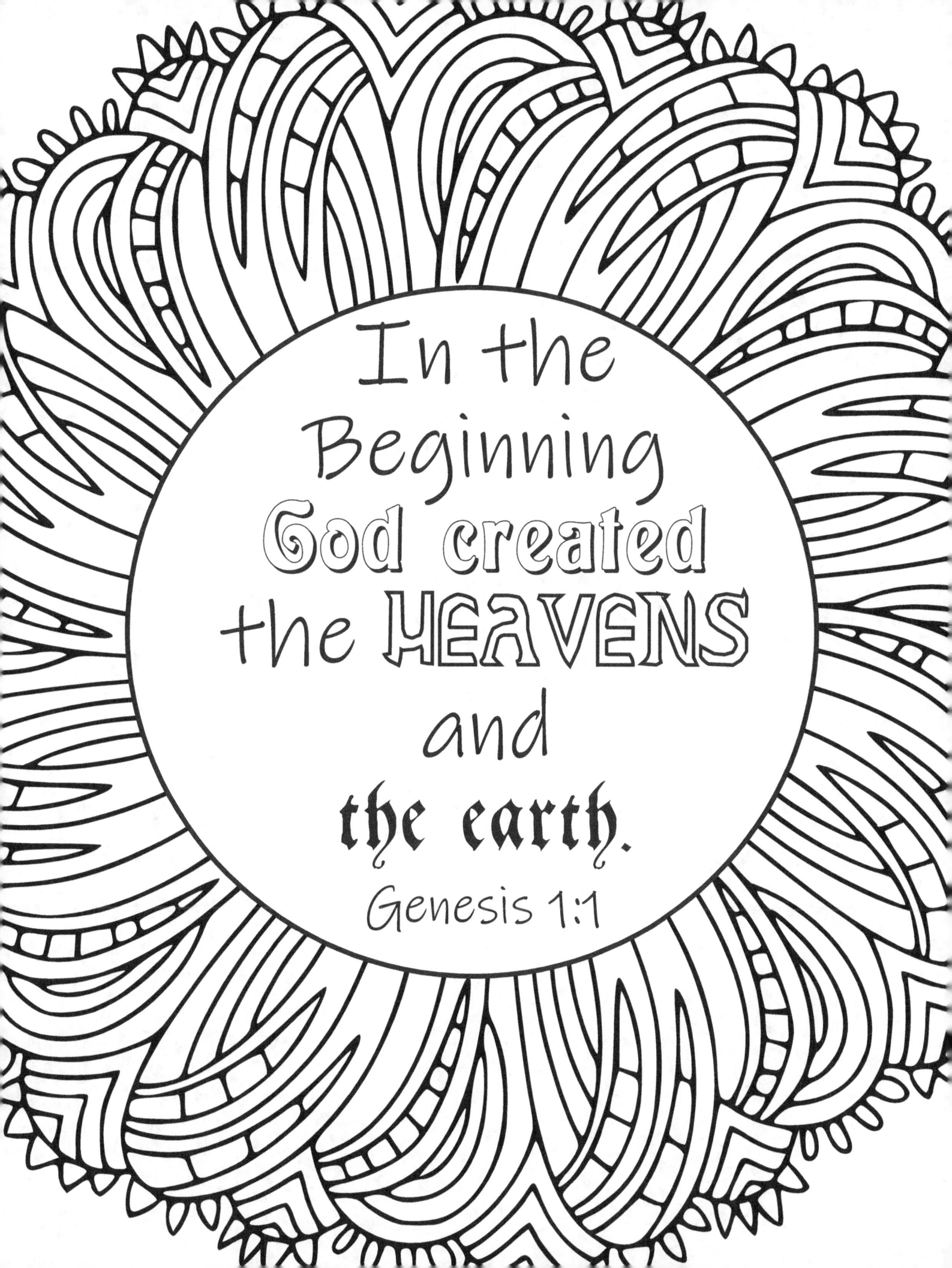

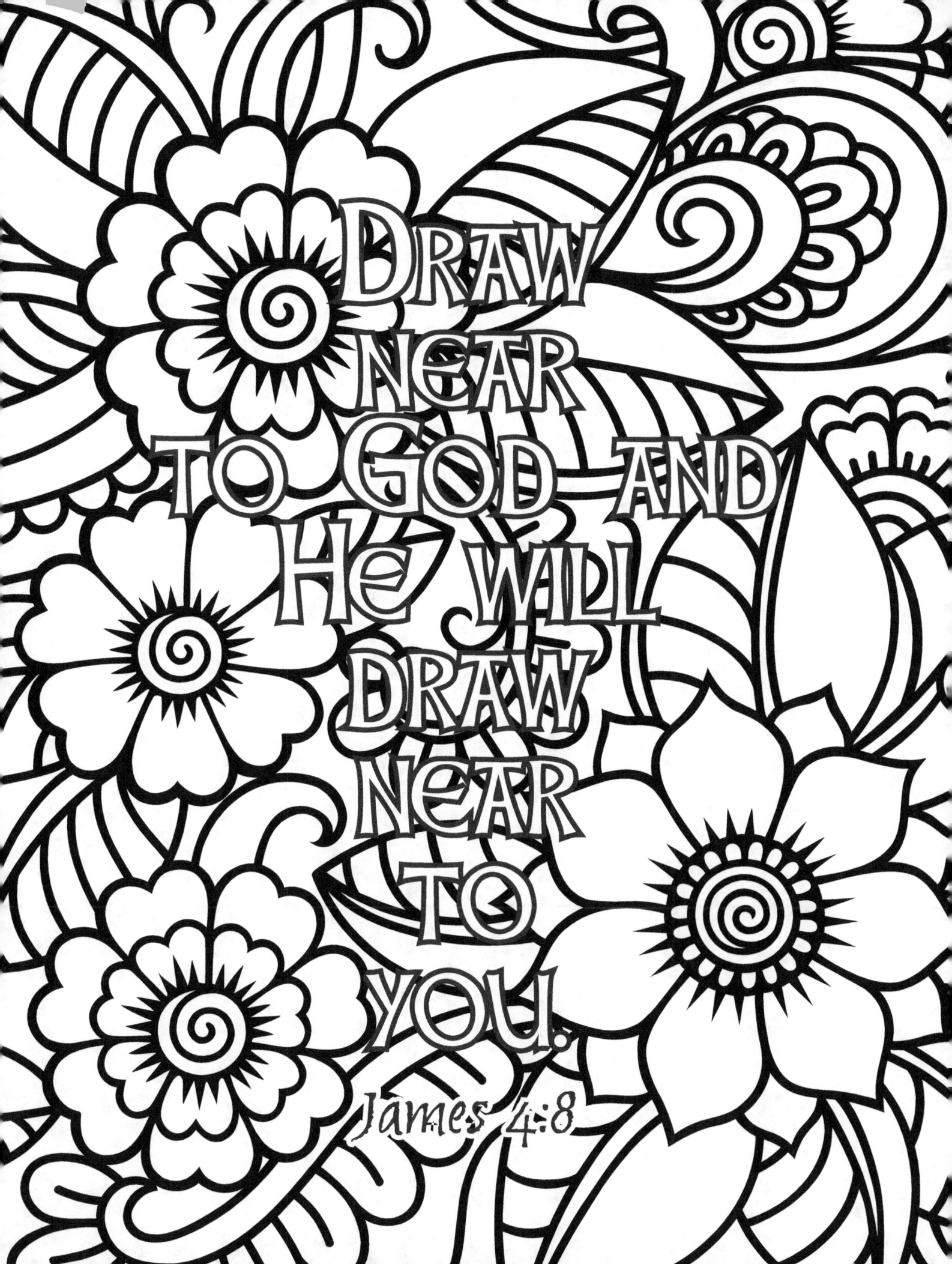

Delight yourself also in the Lord, And He shall give you the desires of your heart. Psalm 37:4

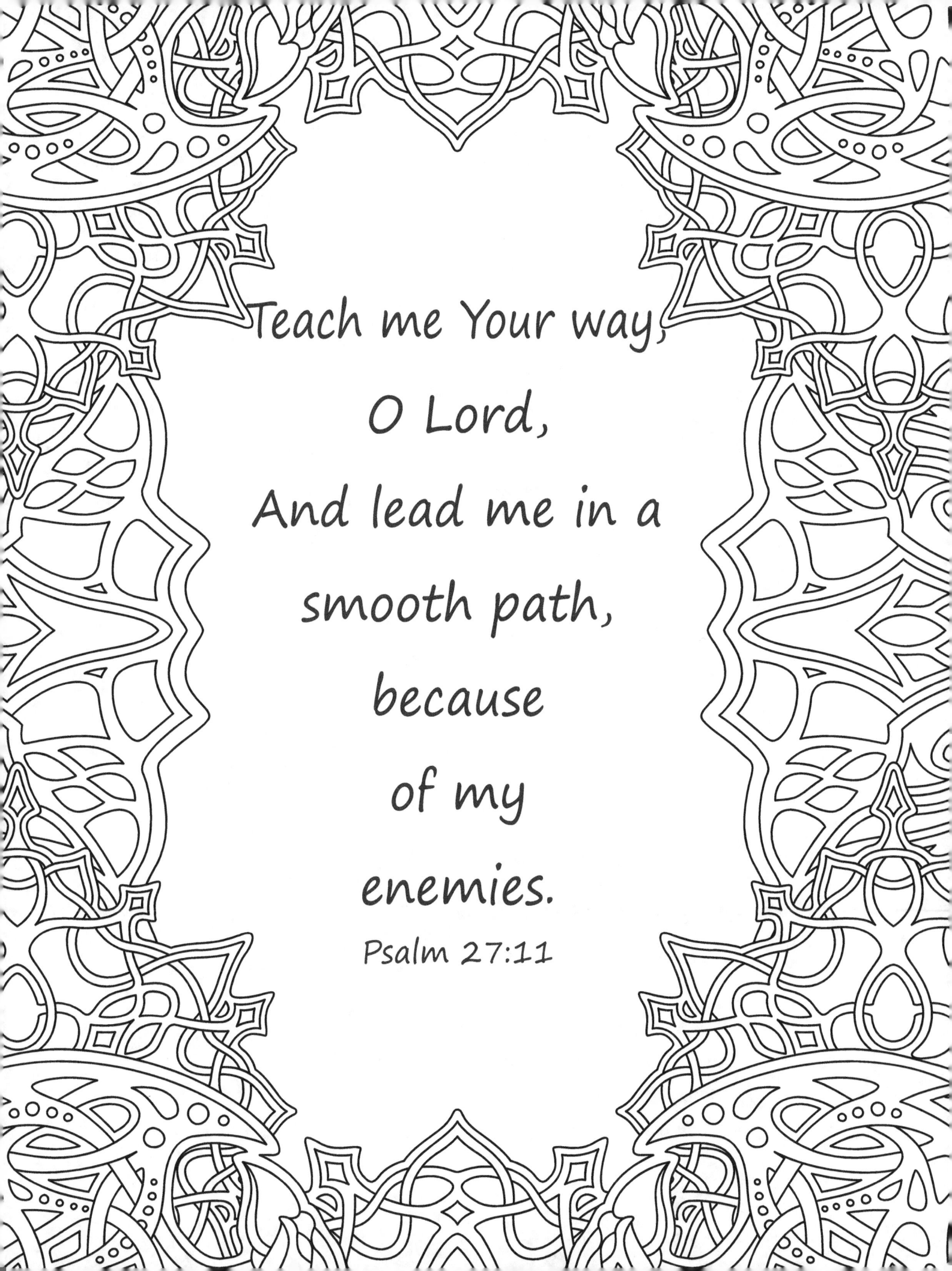

Teach me Your way,
O Lord,
And lead me in a
smooth path,
because
of my
enemies.
Psalm 27:11

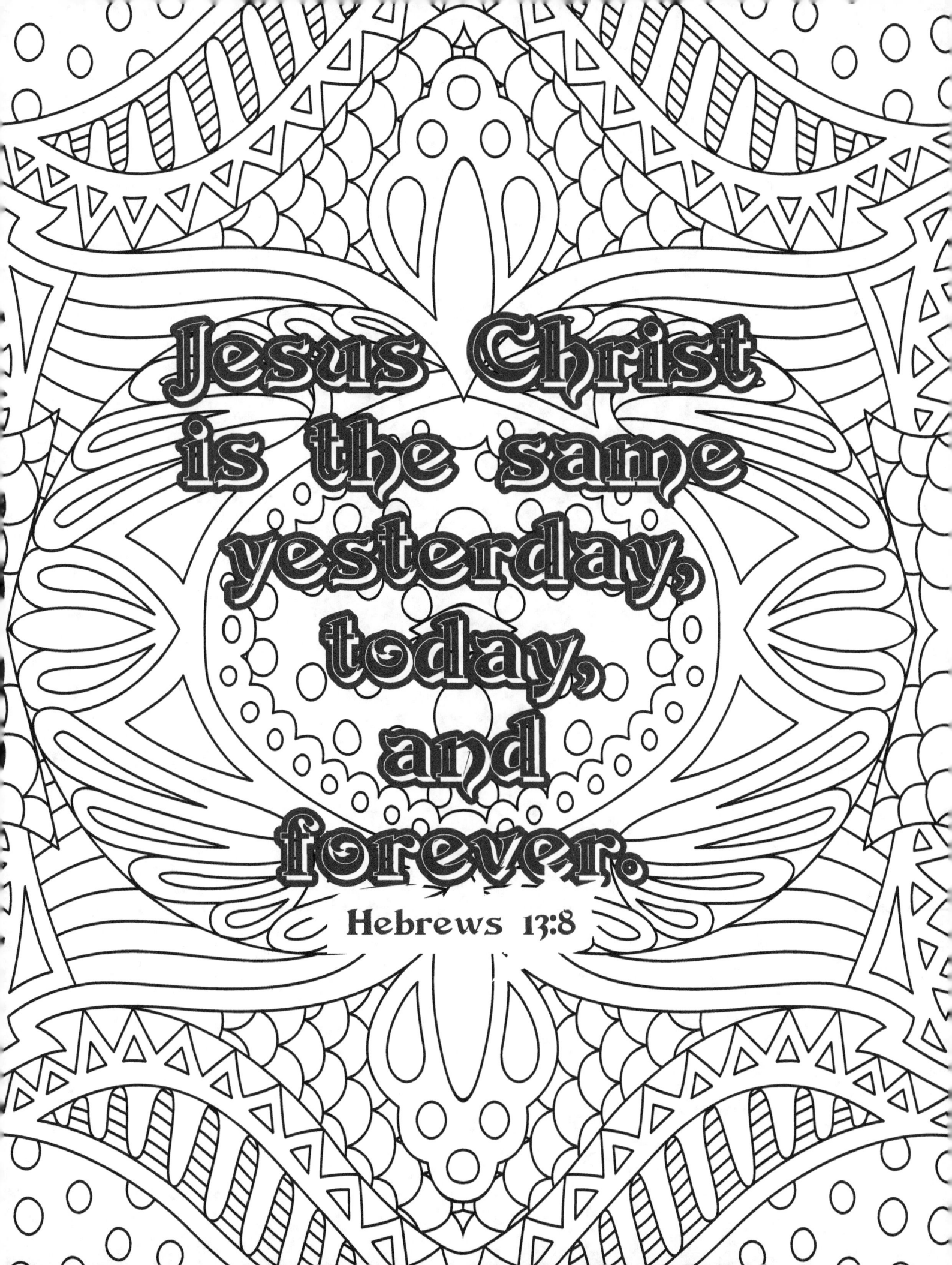

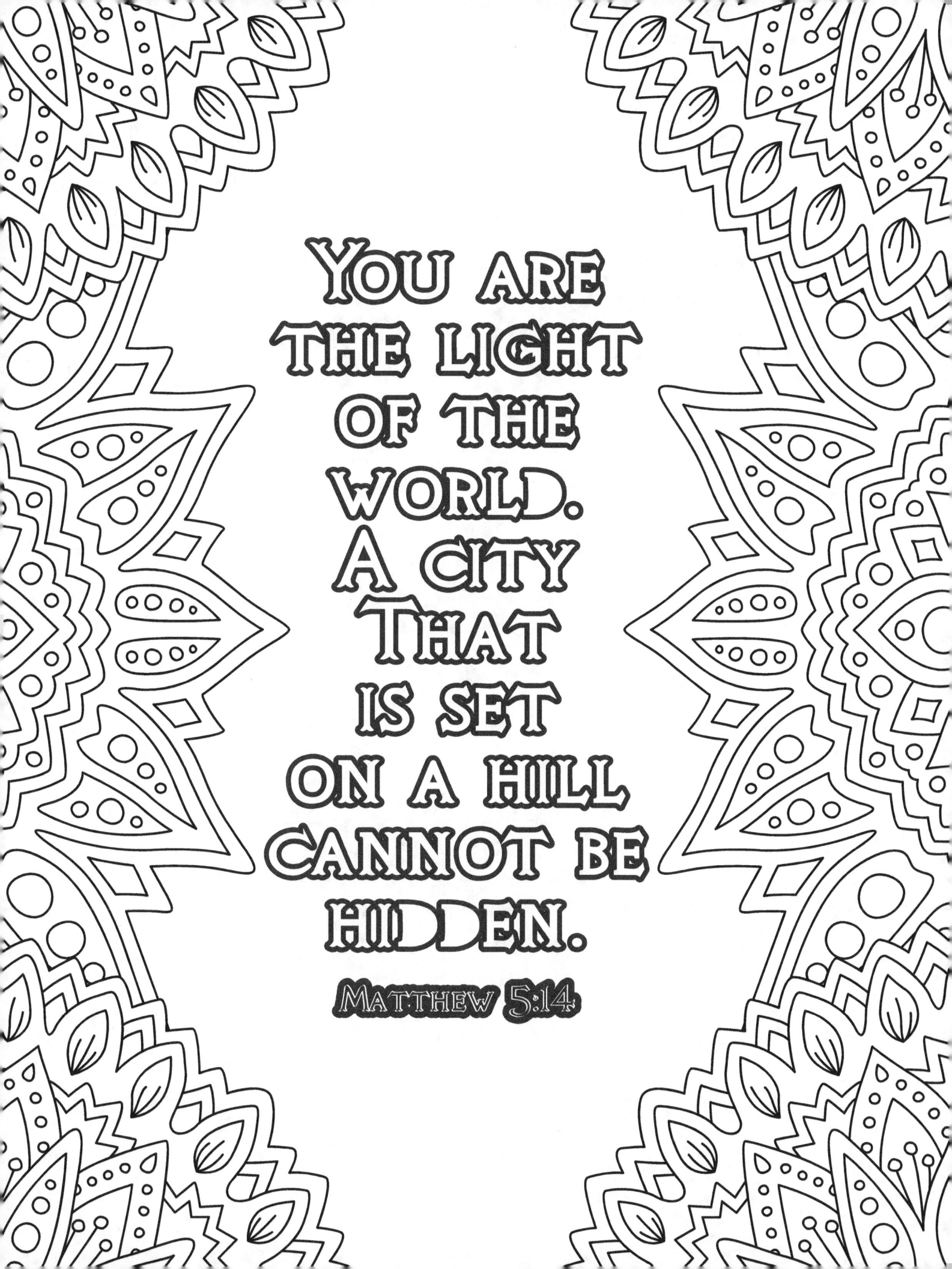

You are the light of the world. A city that is set on a hill cannot be hidden.

Matthew 5:14

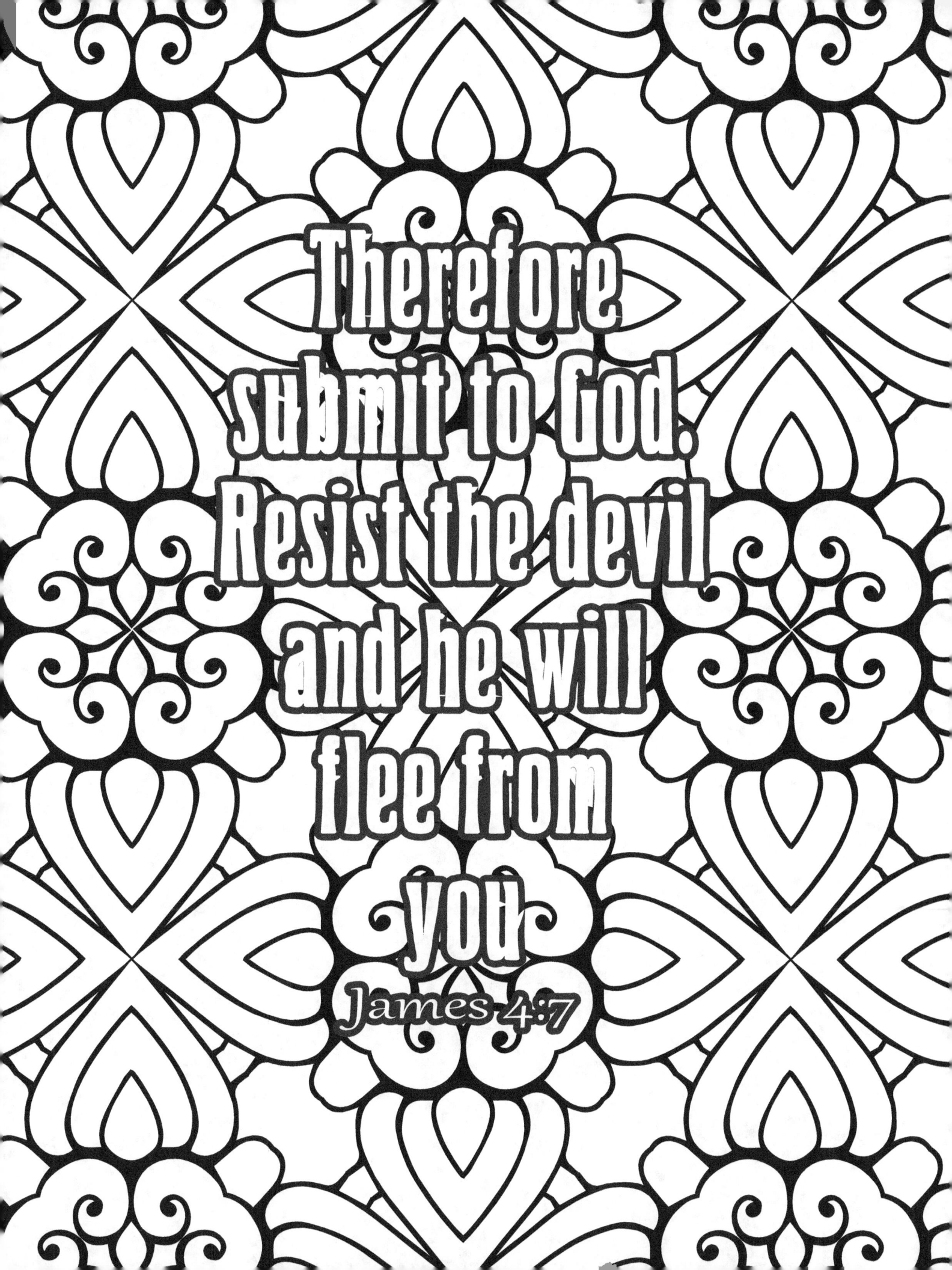

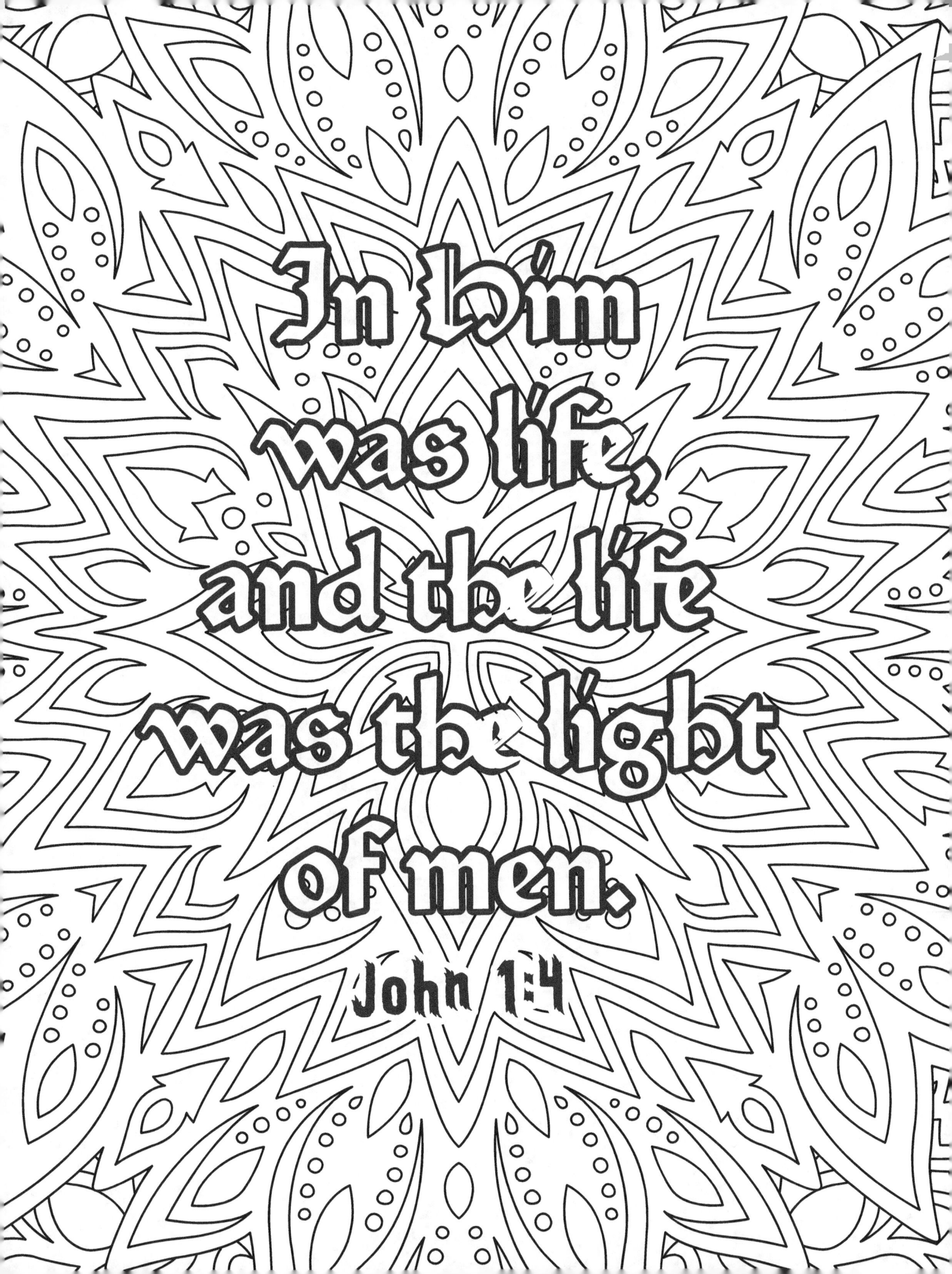

In Him was life, and the life was the light of men.

John 1:4

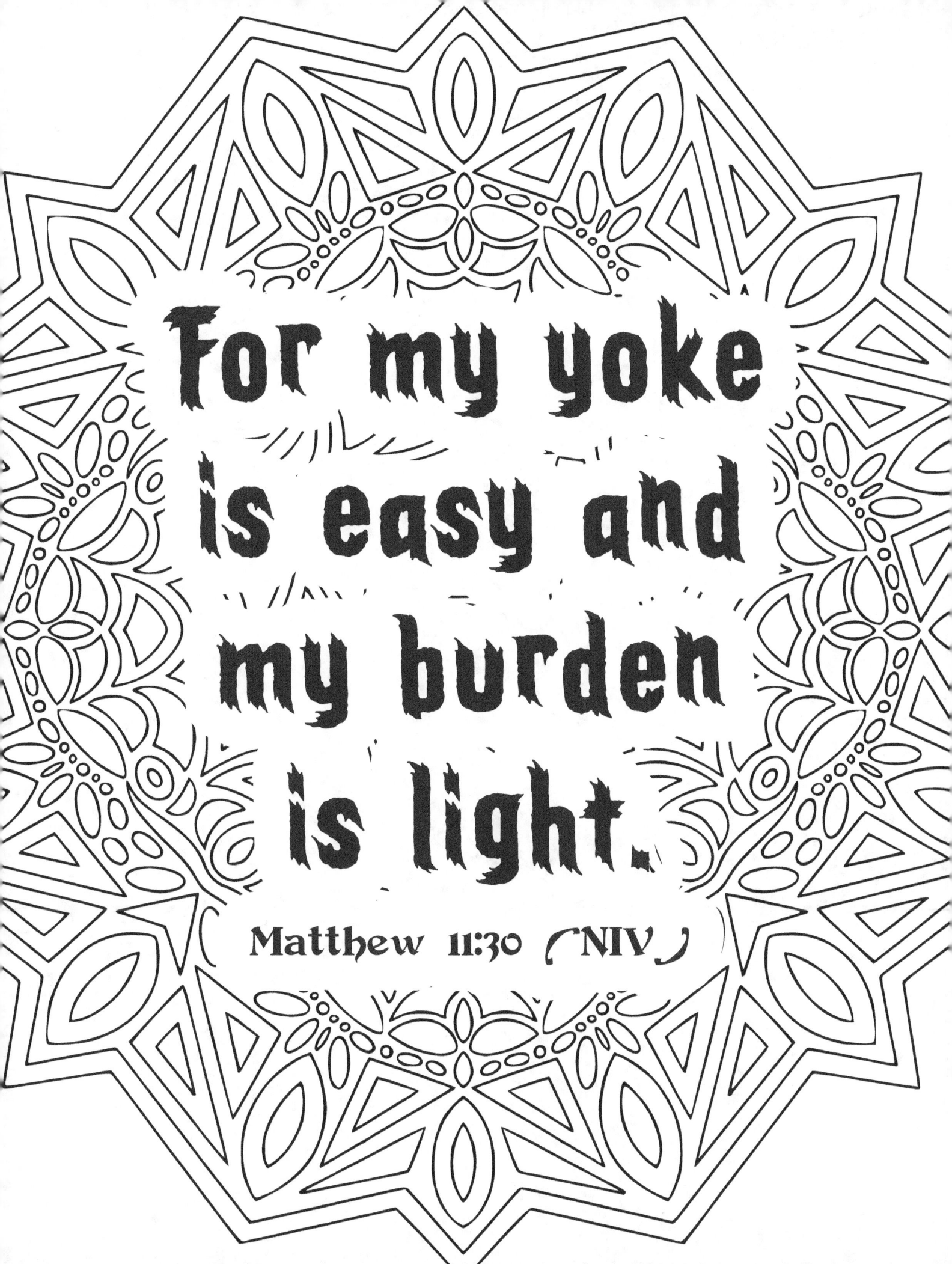

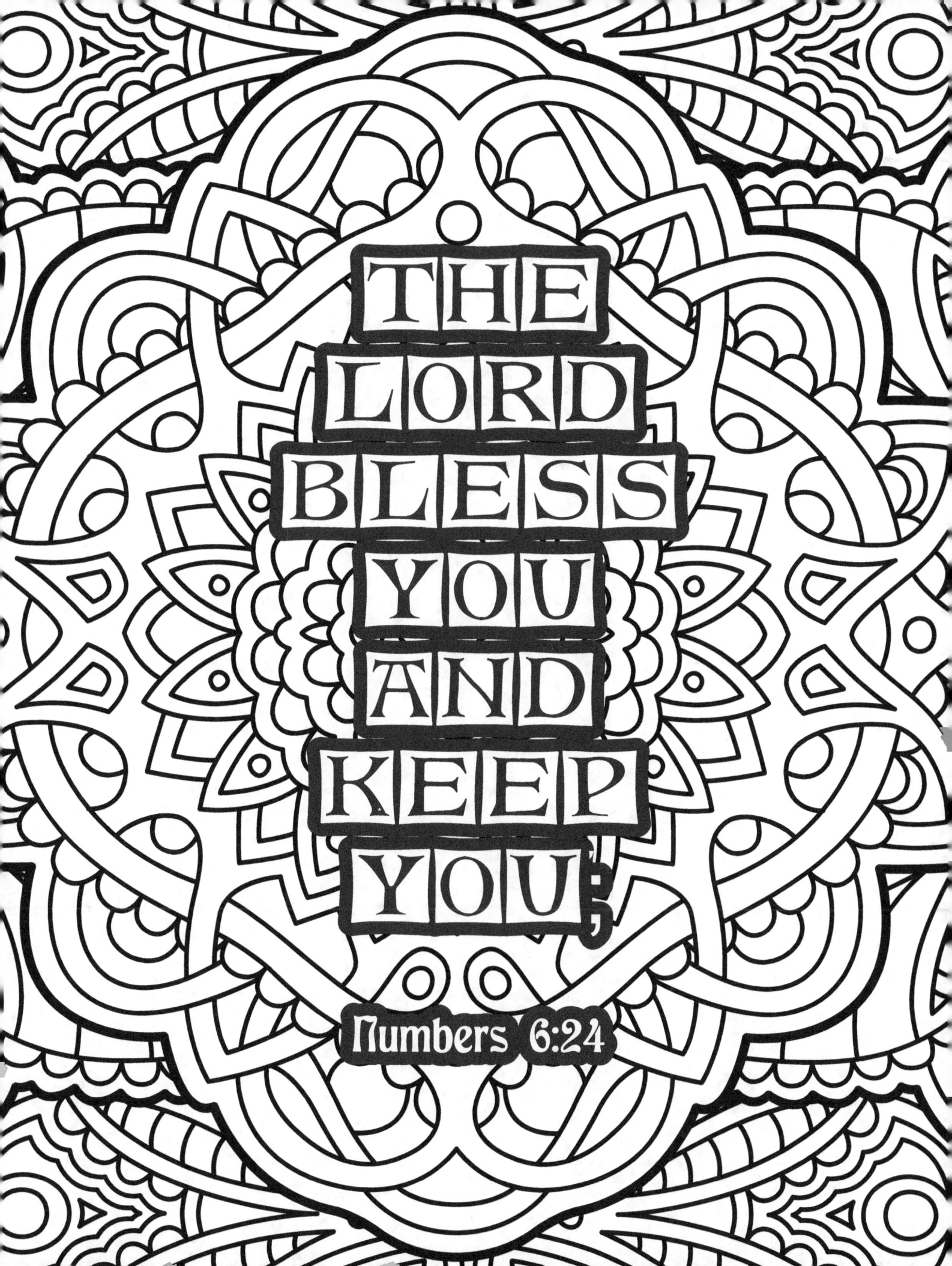

The name of the Lord is a strong tower; The righteous run to it and are safe

Proverbs 18:10

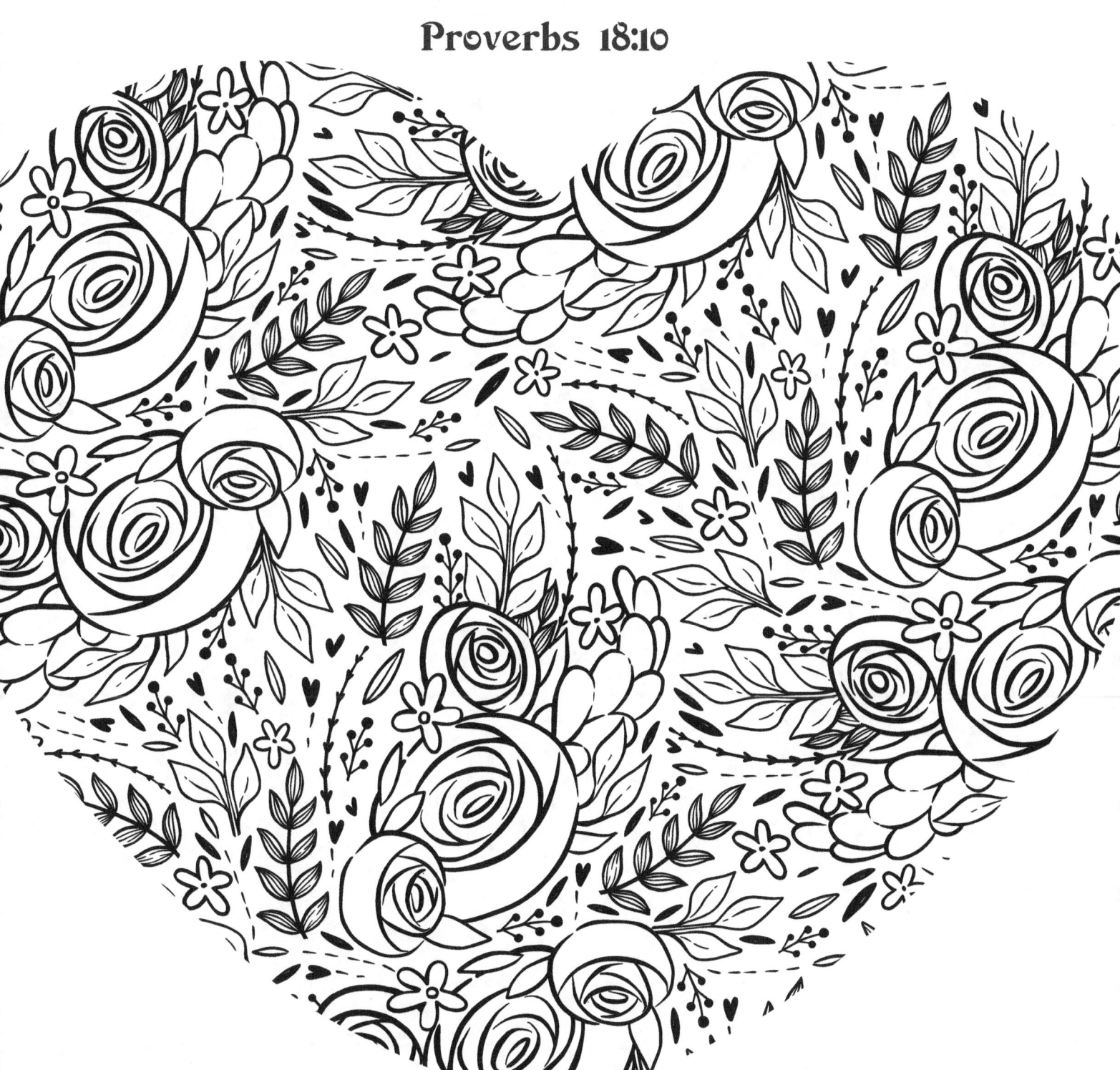

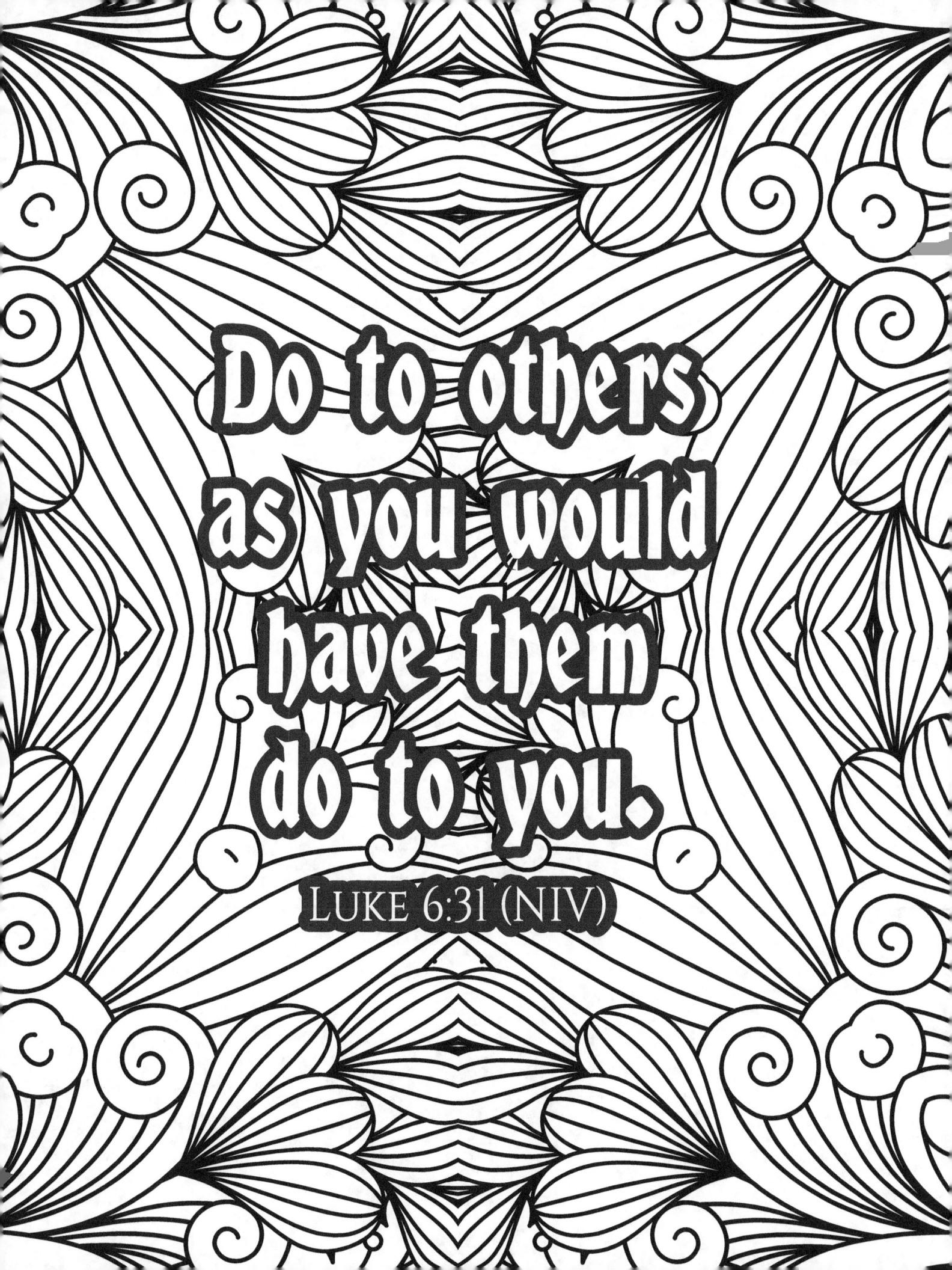

Oh, give thanks to the *Lord*, for He is *good*! For His mercy endures *forever*.

Psalm 136:1

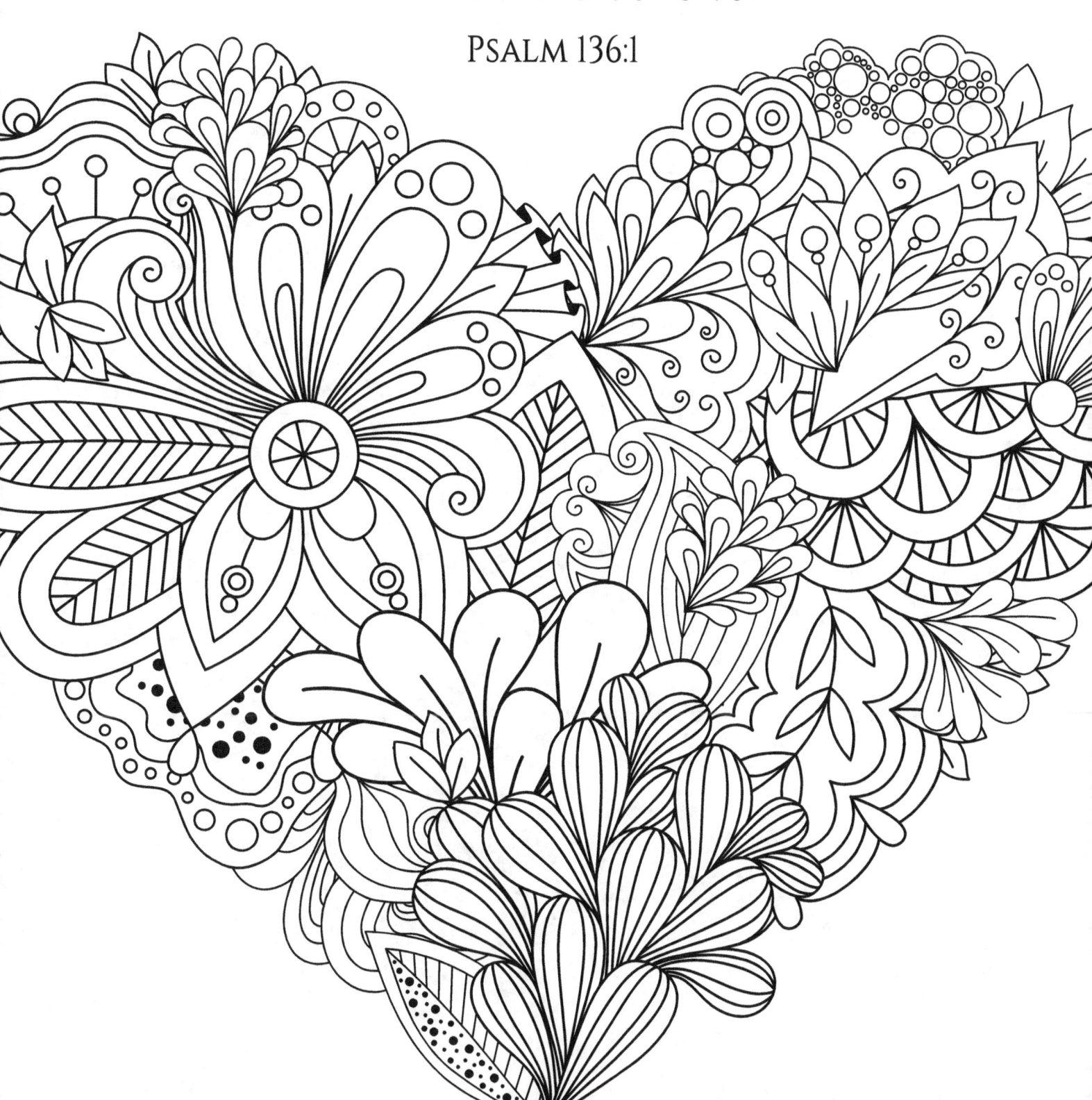

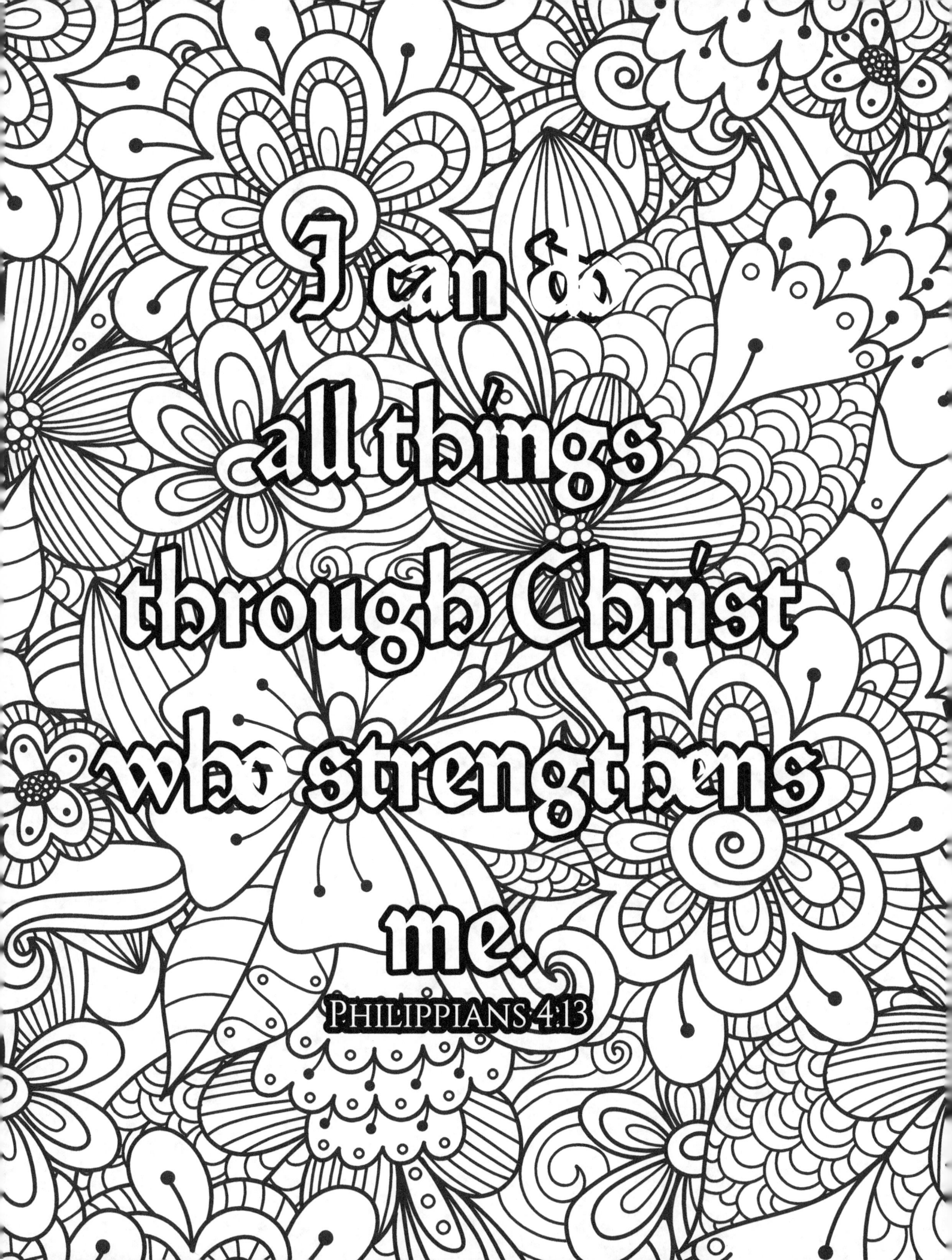

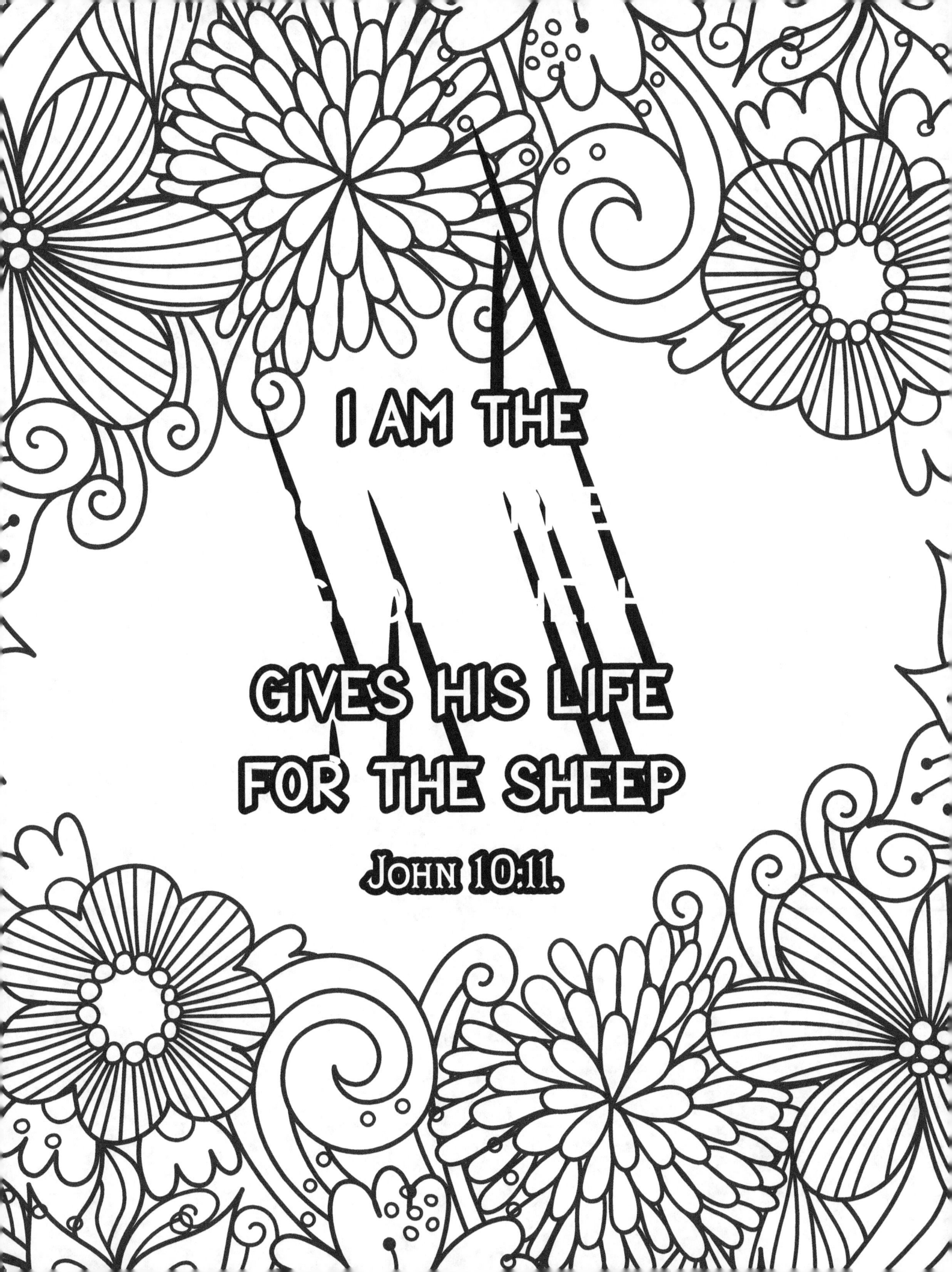

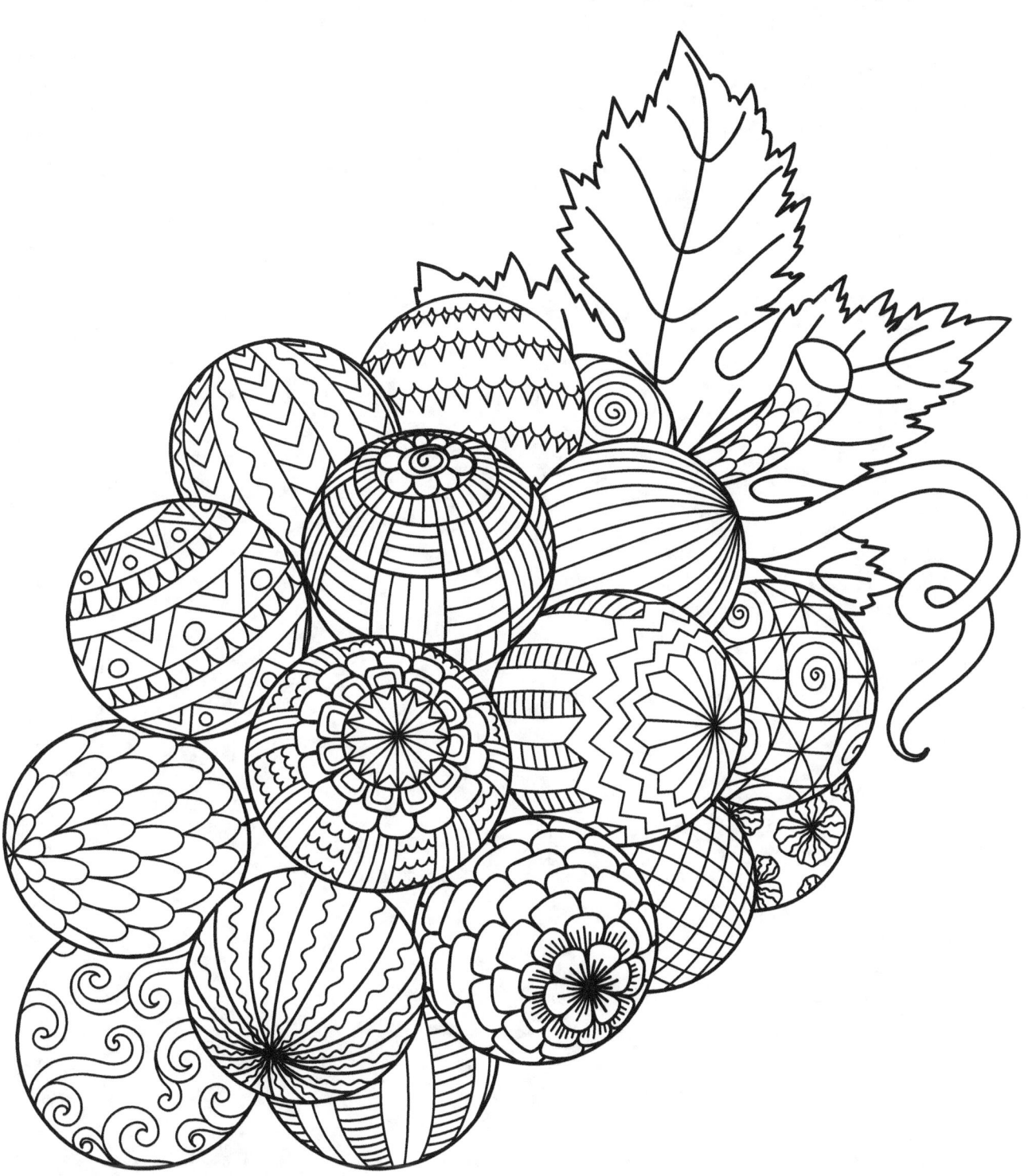

Commit your way to the Lord,
Trust also in Him,
And He shall bring it to pass.

Psalm 37:5

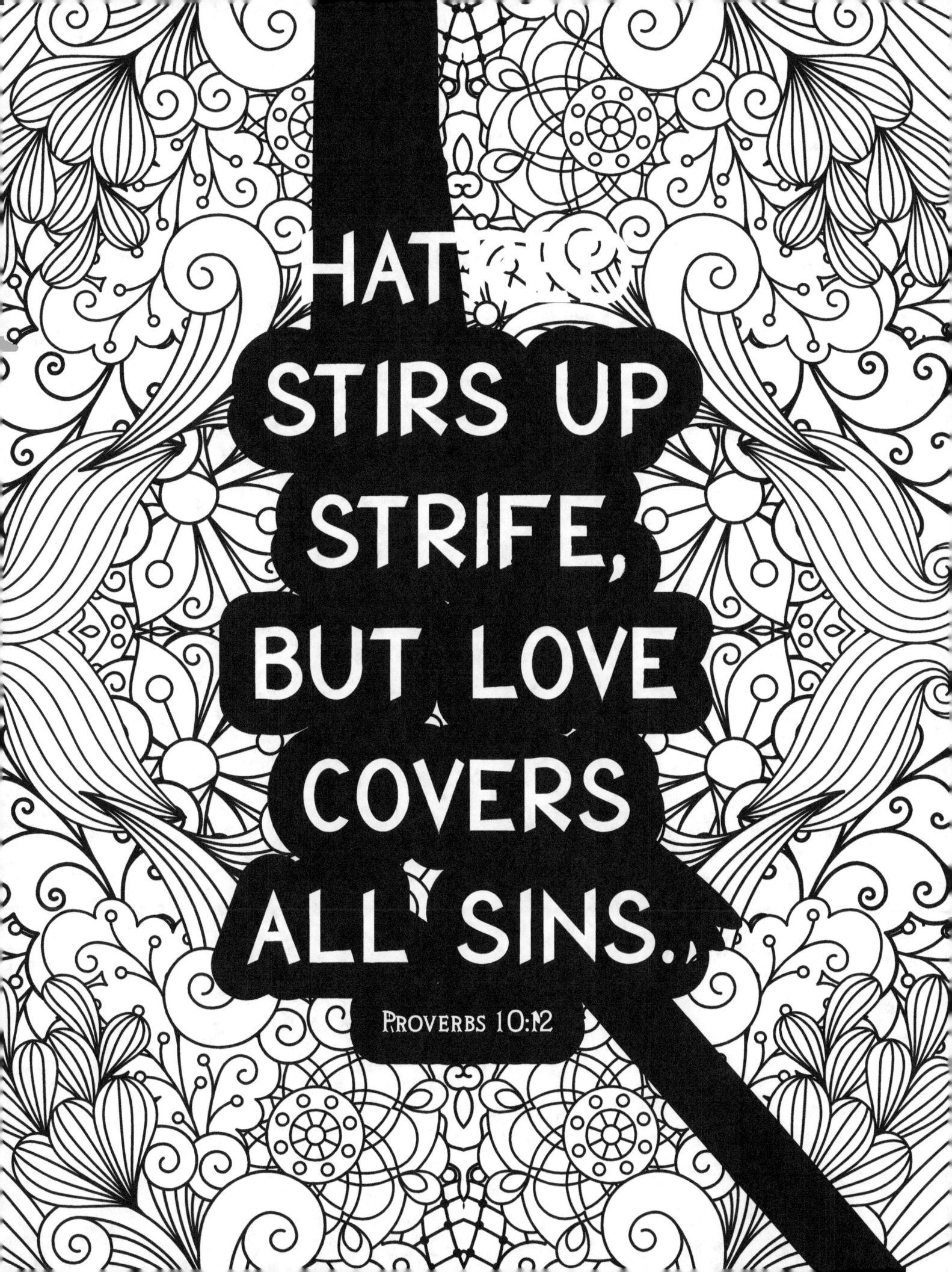

HAT STIRS UP STRIFE, BUT LOVE COVERS ALL SINS.

PROVERBS 10:12

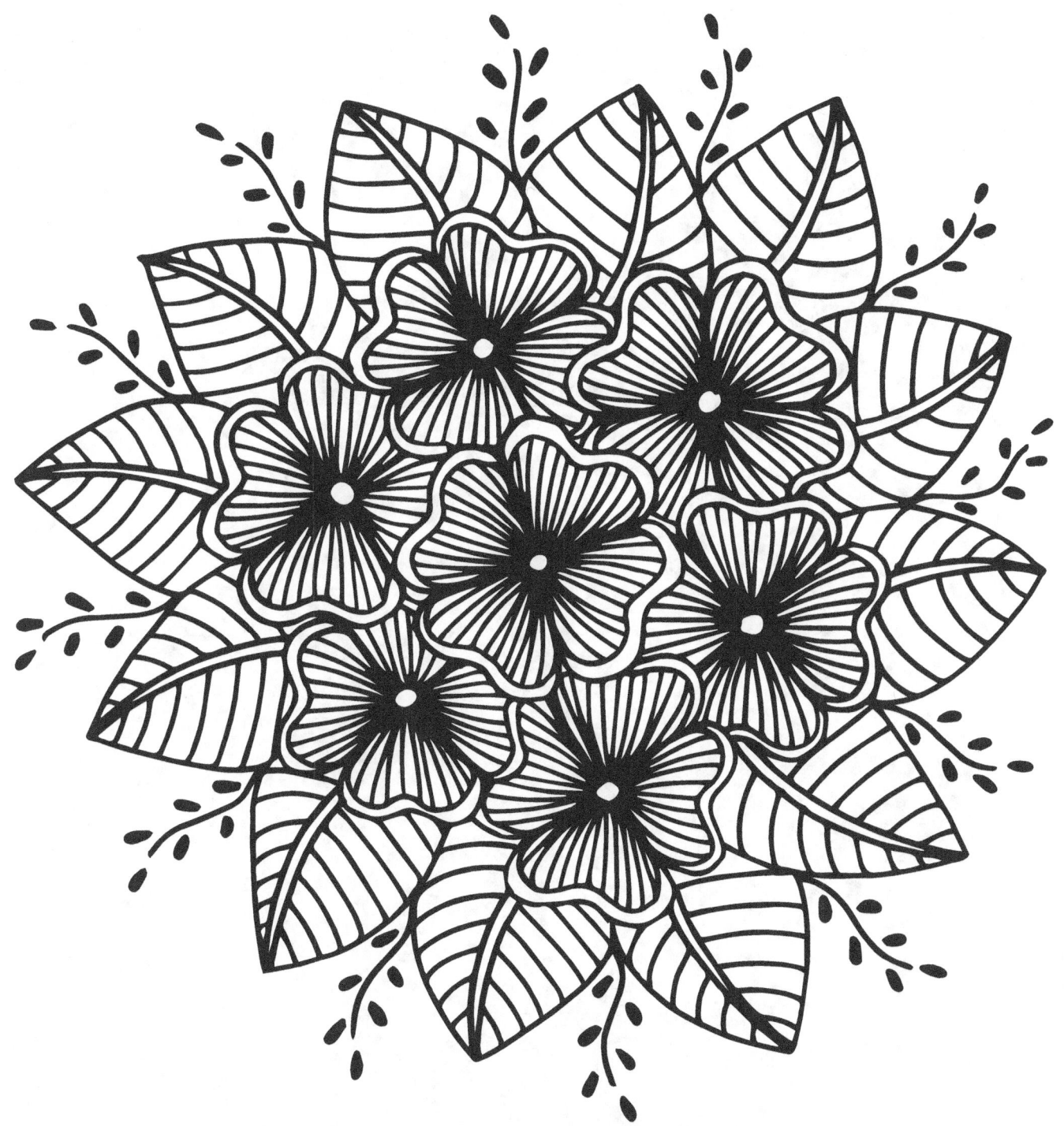

REJOICING IN HOPE,
PATIENT IN TRIBULATION,
CONTINUING STEADFASTLY
IN PRAYER

Romans 12:12

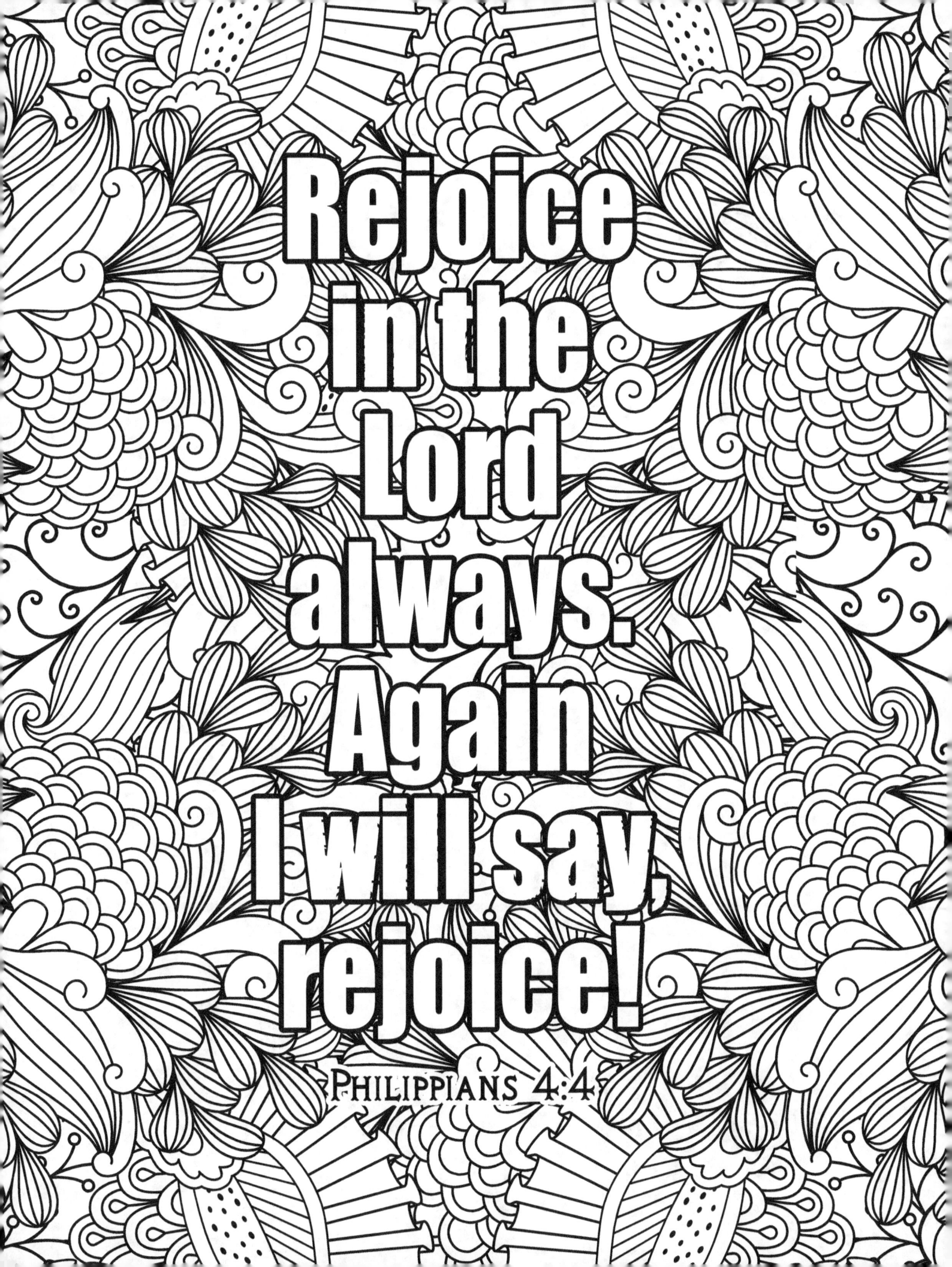

Rejoice in the Lord always. Again I will say, rejoice!

PHILIPPIANS 4:4

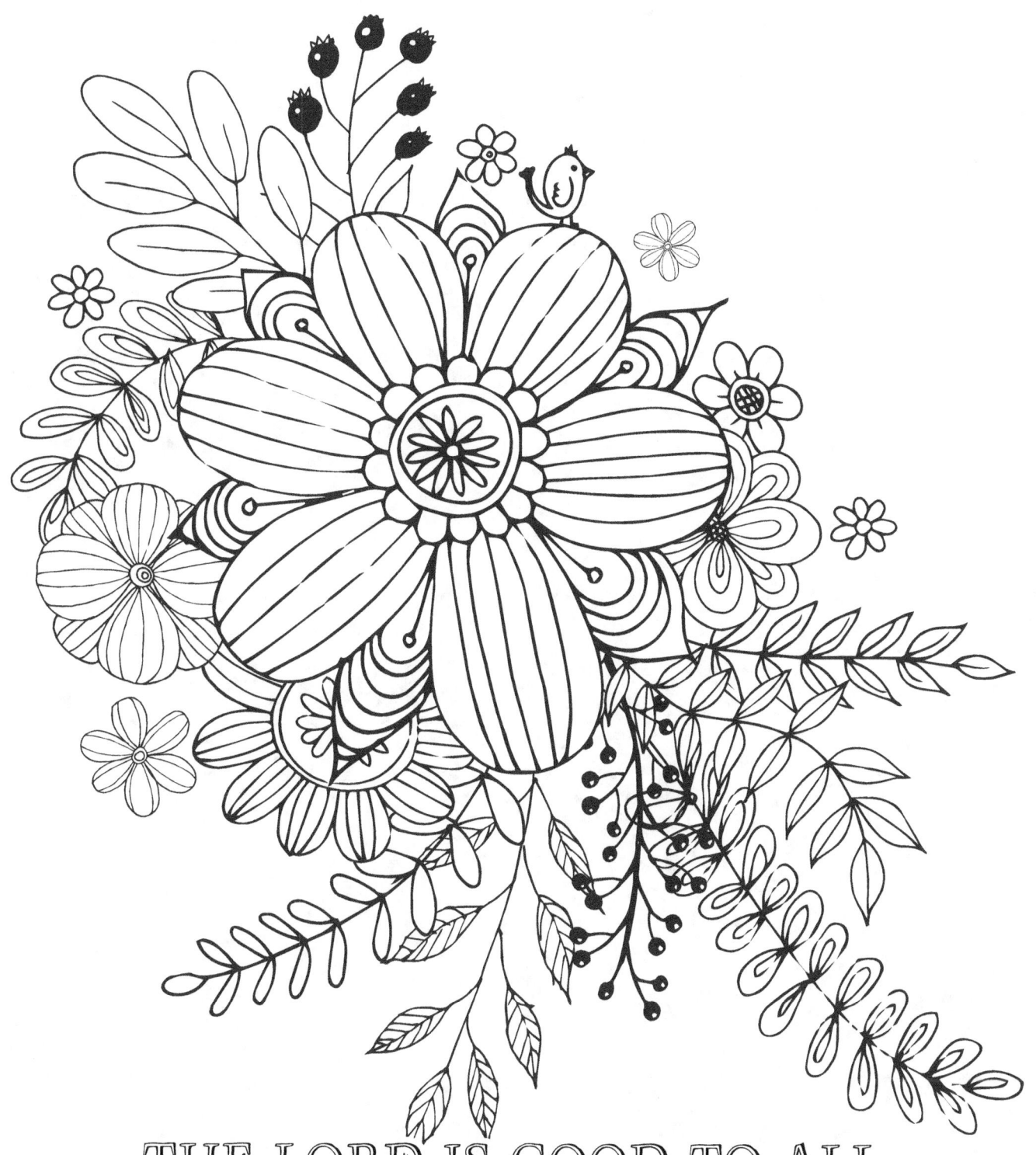

THE LORD IS GOOD TO ALL,
AND HIS TENDER
MERCIES ARE OVER
ALL HIS WORKS.

PSALM 145:9

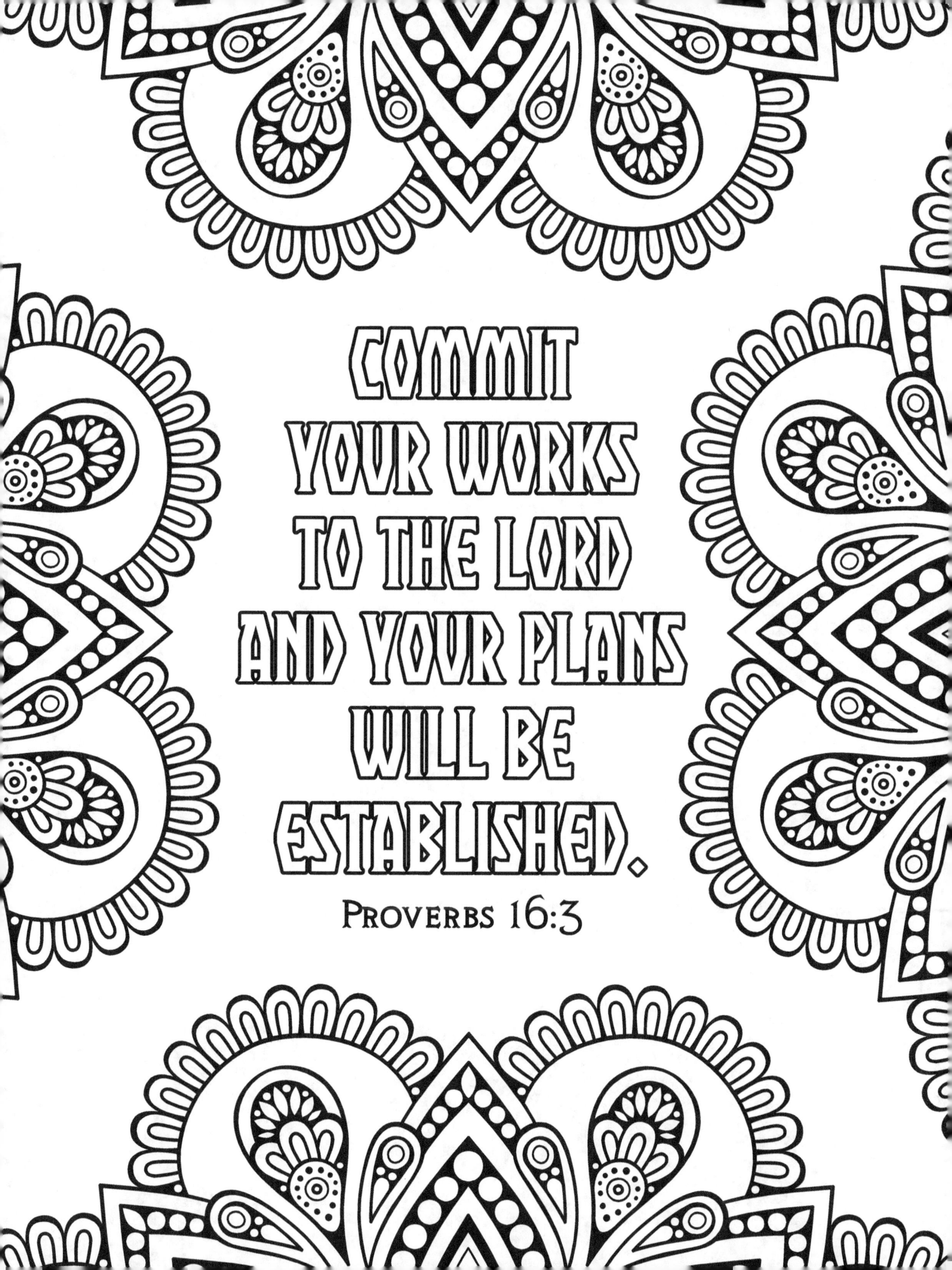

COMMIT YOUR WORKS TO THE LORD AND YOUR PLANS WILL BE ESTABLISHED.

Proverbs 16:3

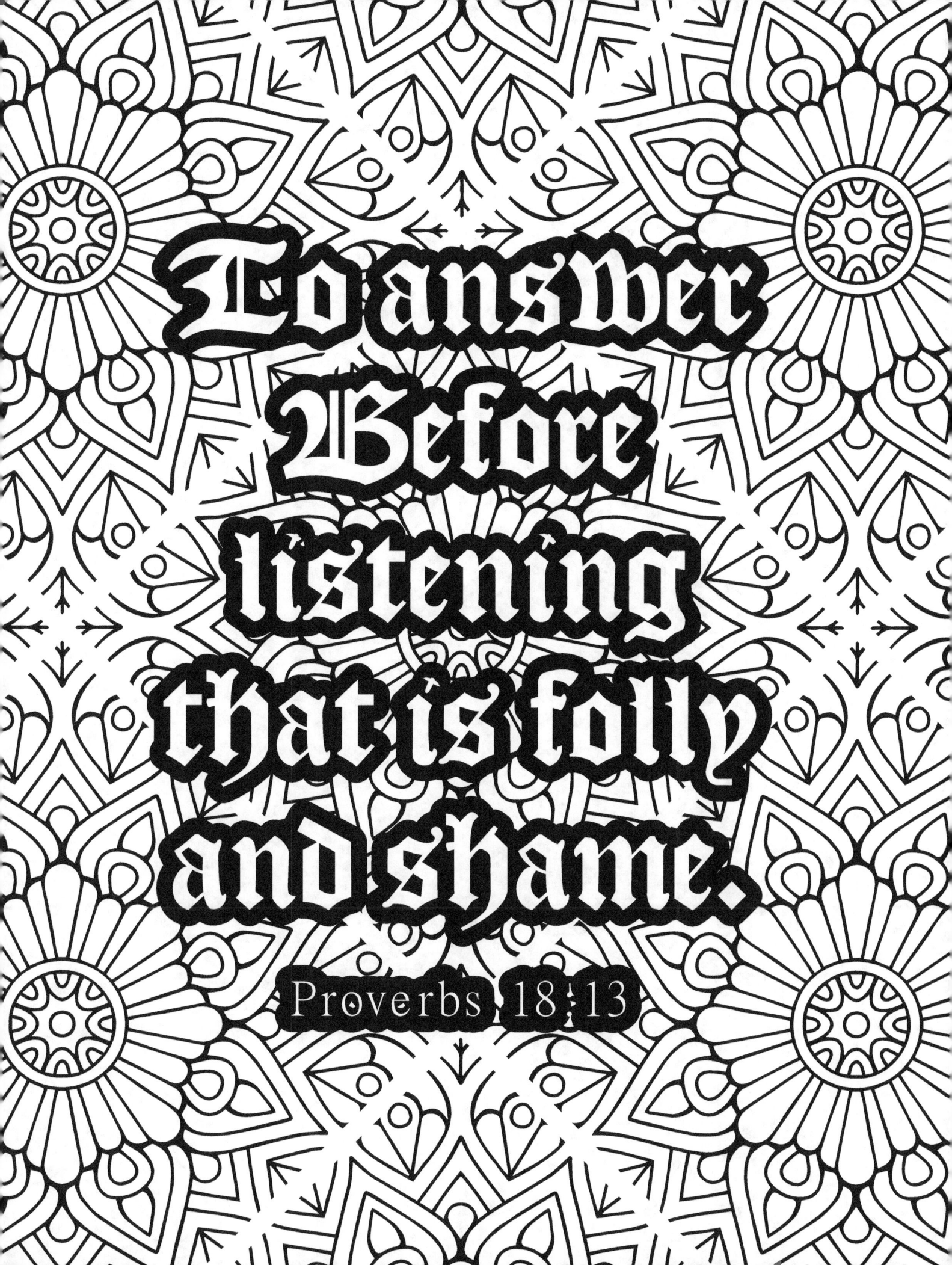

To answer
Before
listening
that is folly
and shame.

Proverbs 18:13

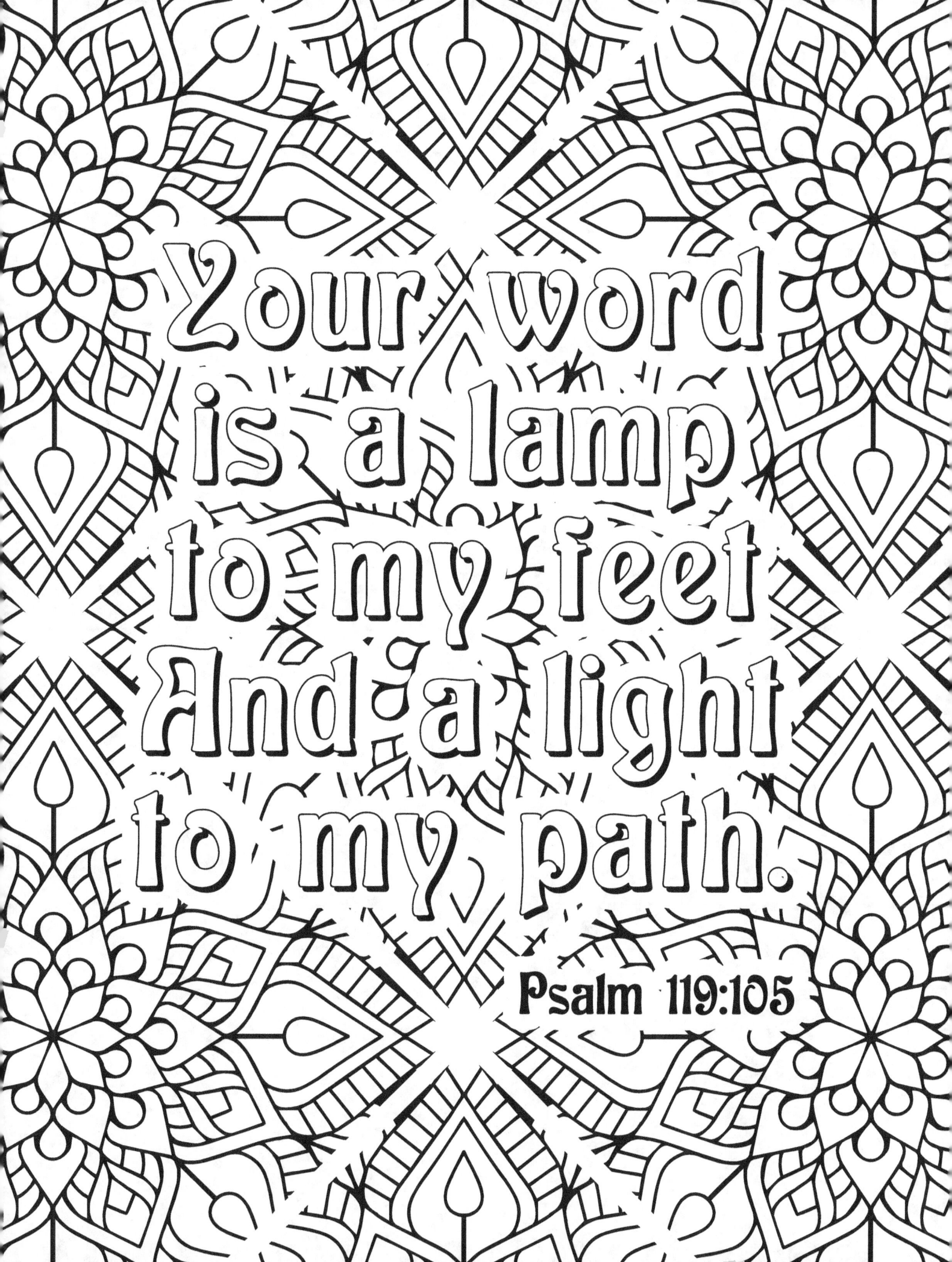

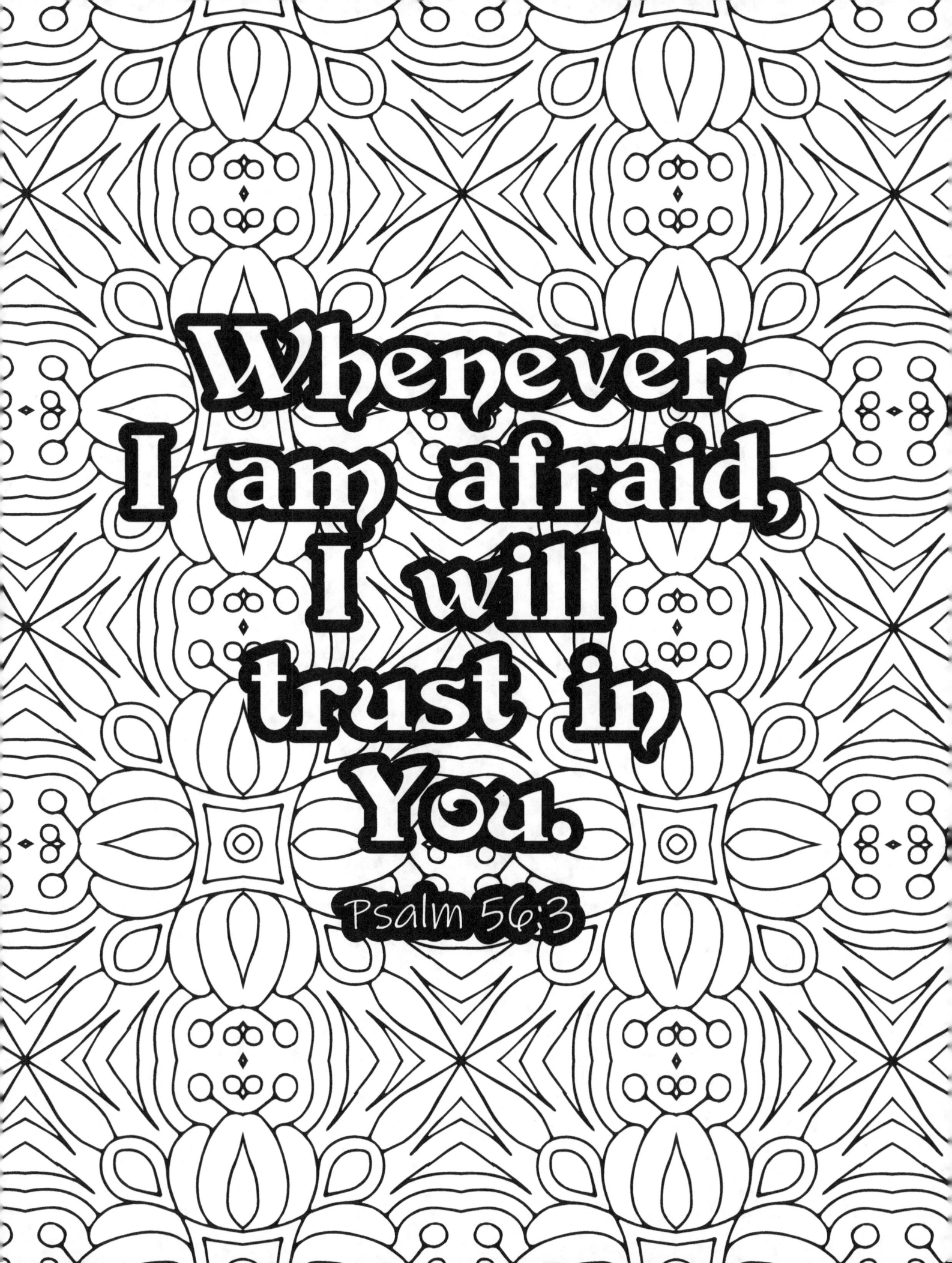

The Lord is my light and my salvation whom shall I fear?

PSALM 27:1

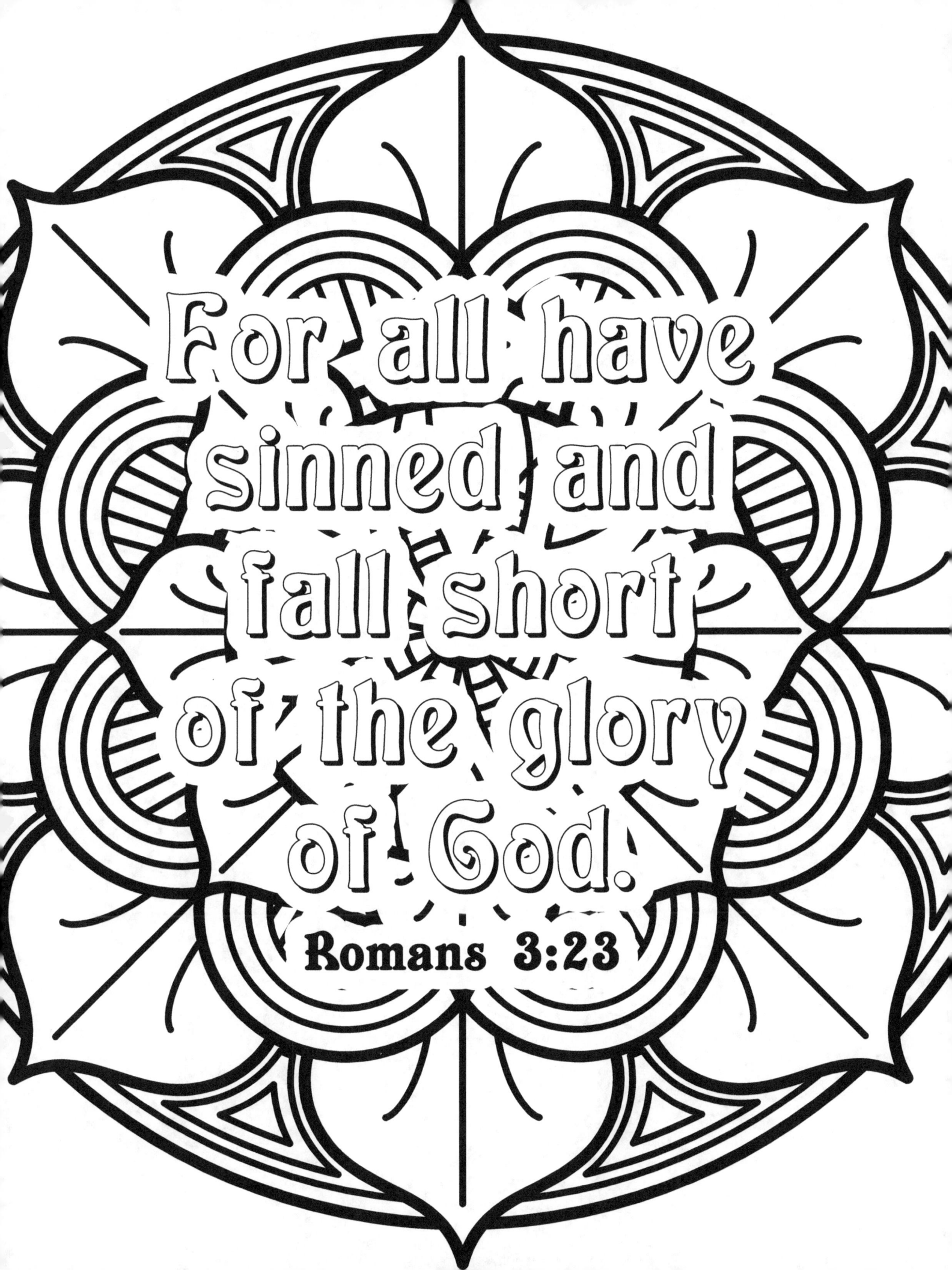

This is the day
the Lord has made;
We will rejoice and be glad in it.

Psalm 118:24

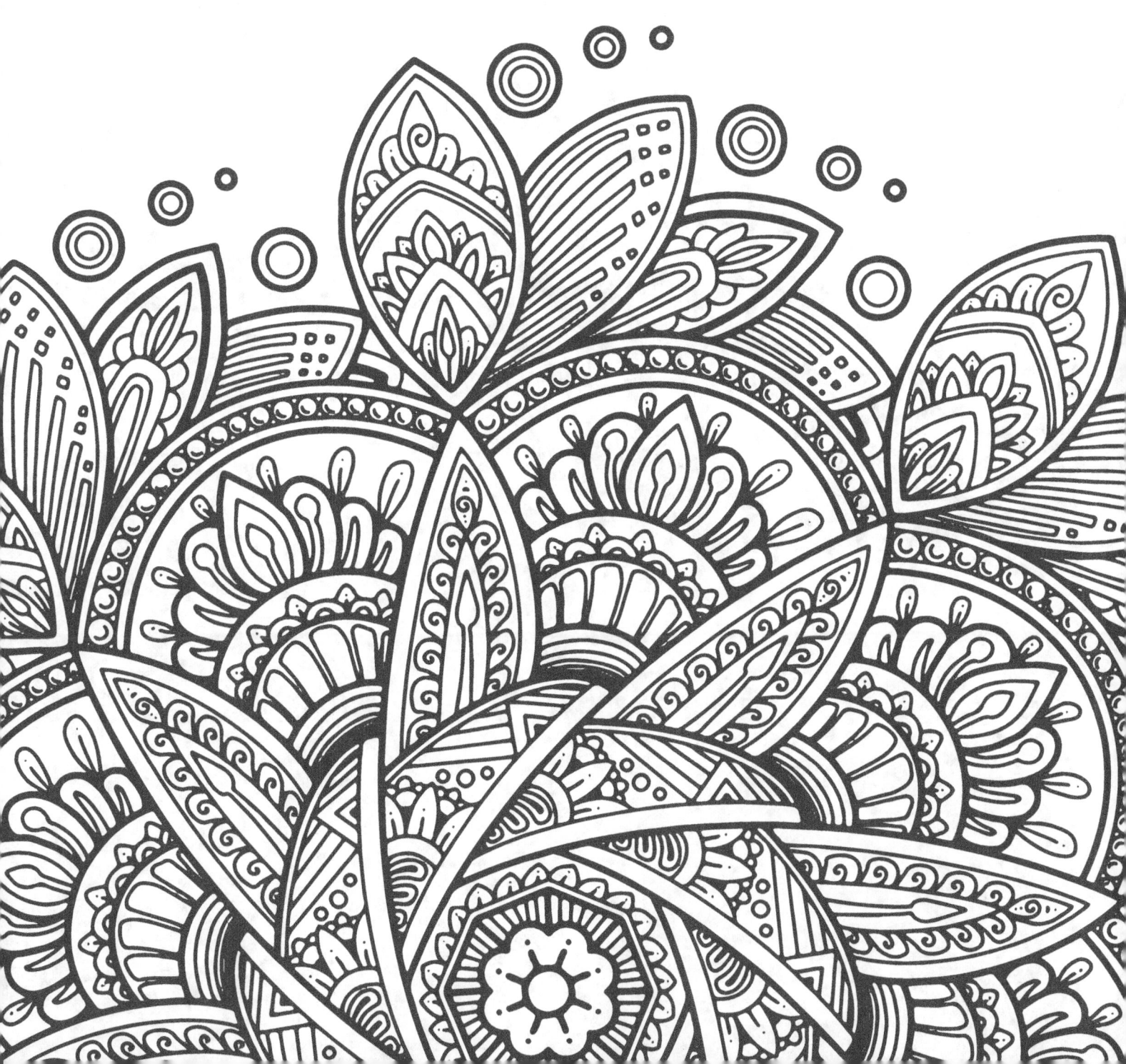

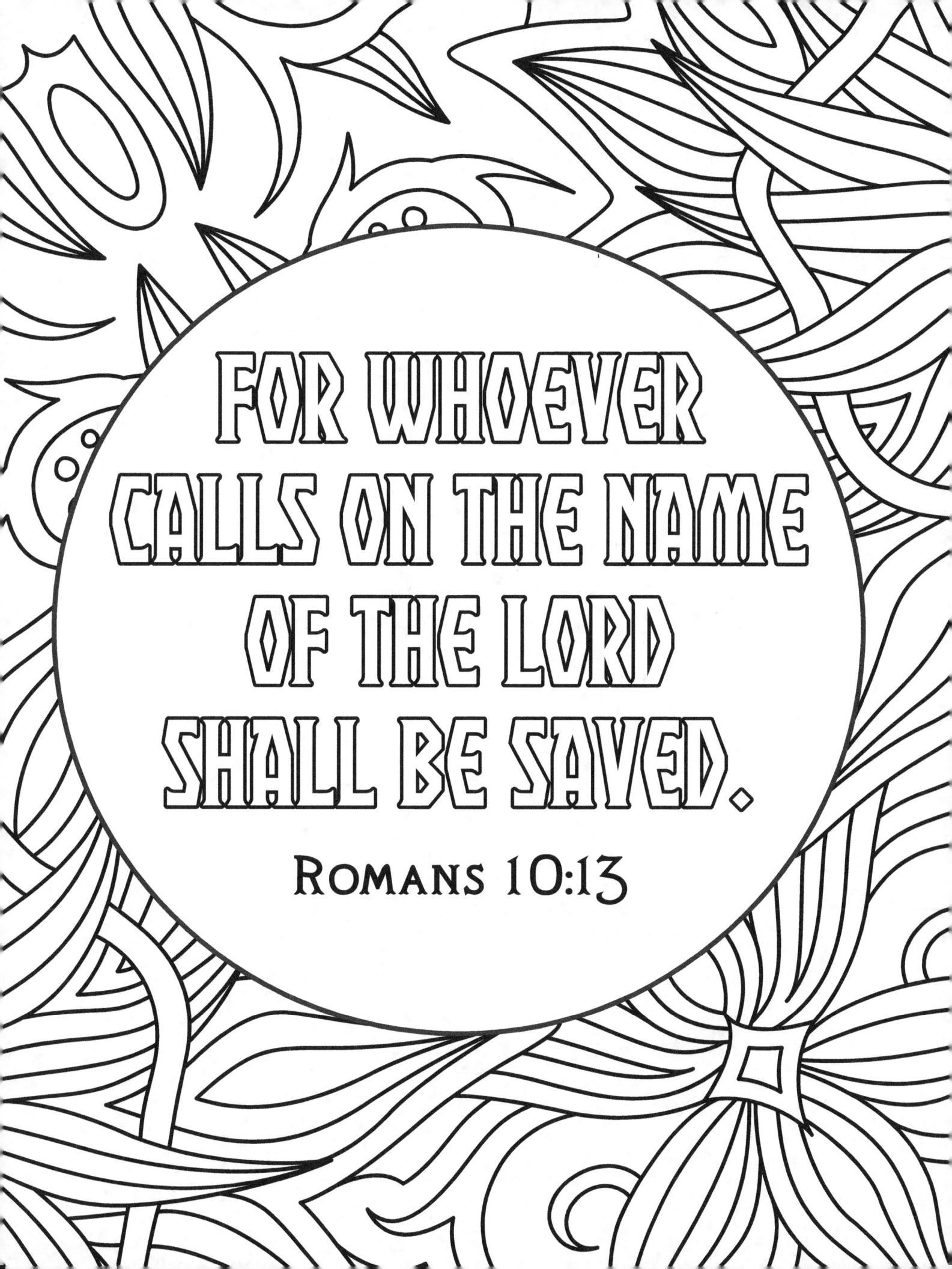

FOR WHOEVER CALLS ON THE NAME OF THE LORD SHALL BE SAVED.

ROMANS 10:13

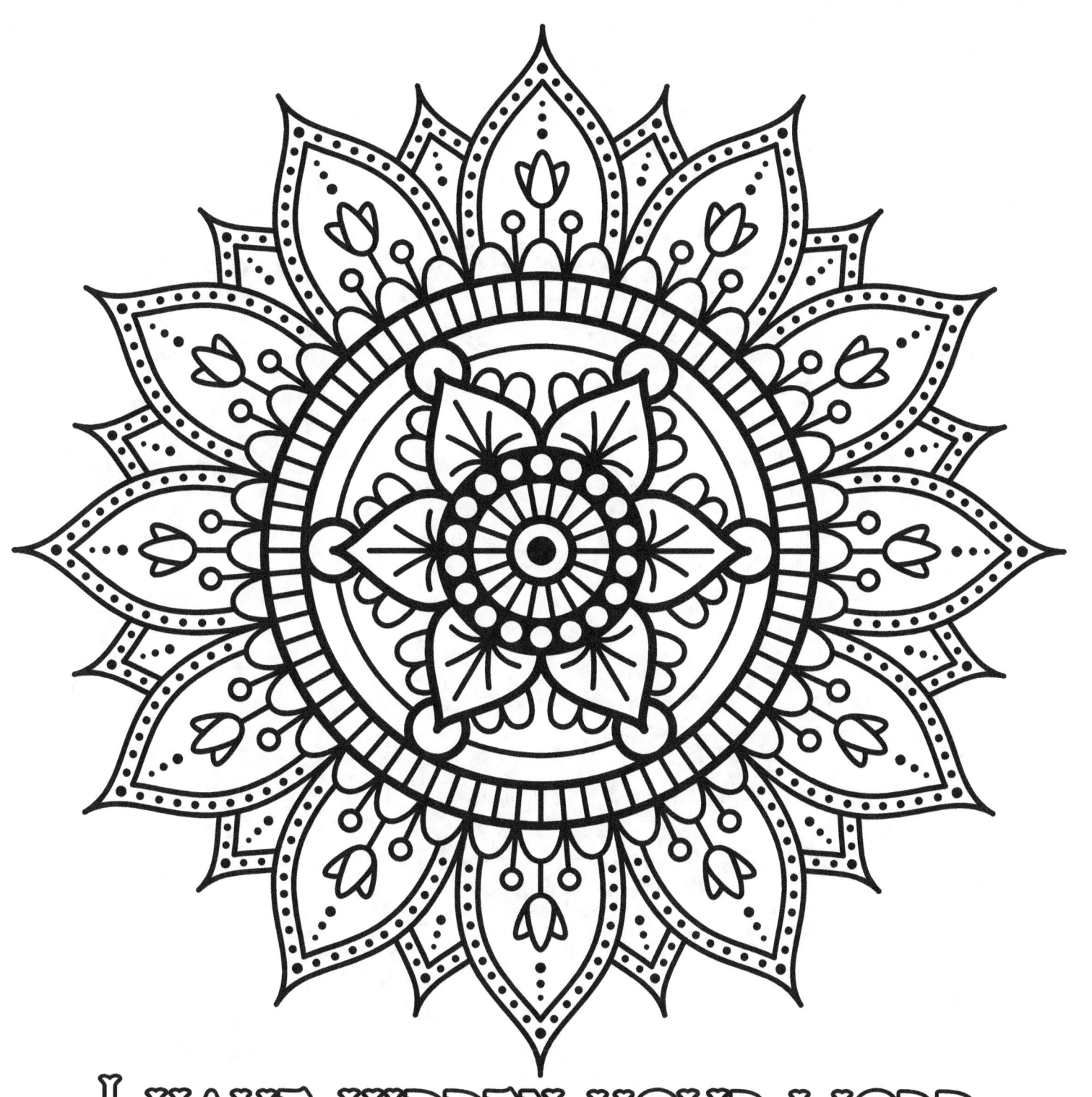

I HAVE HIDDEN YOUR WORD
IN MY HEART
THAT I MIGHT NOT SIN
AGAINST YOU.

Psalm 119:11

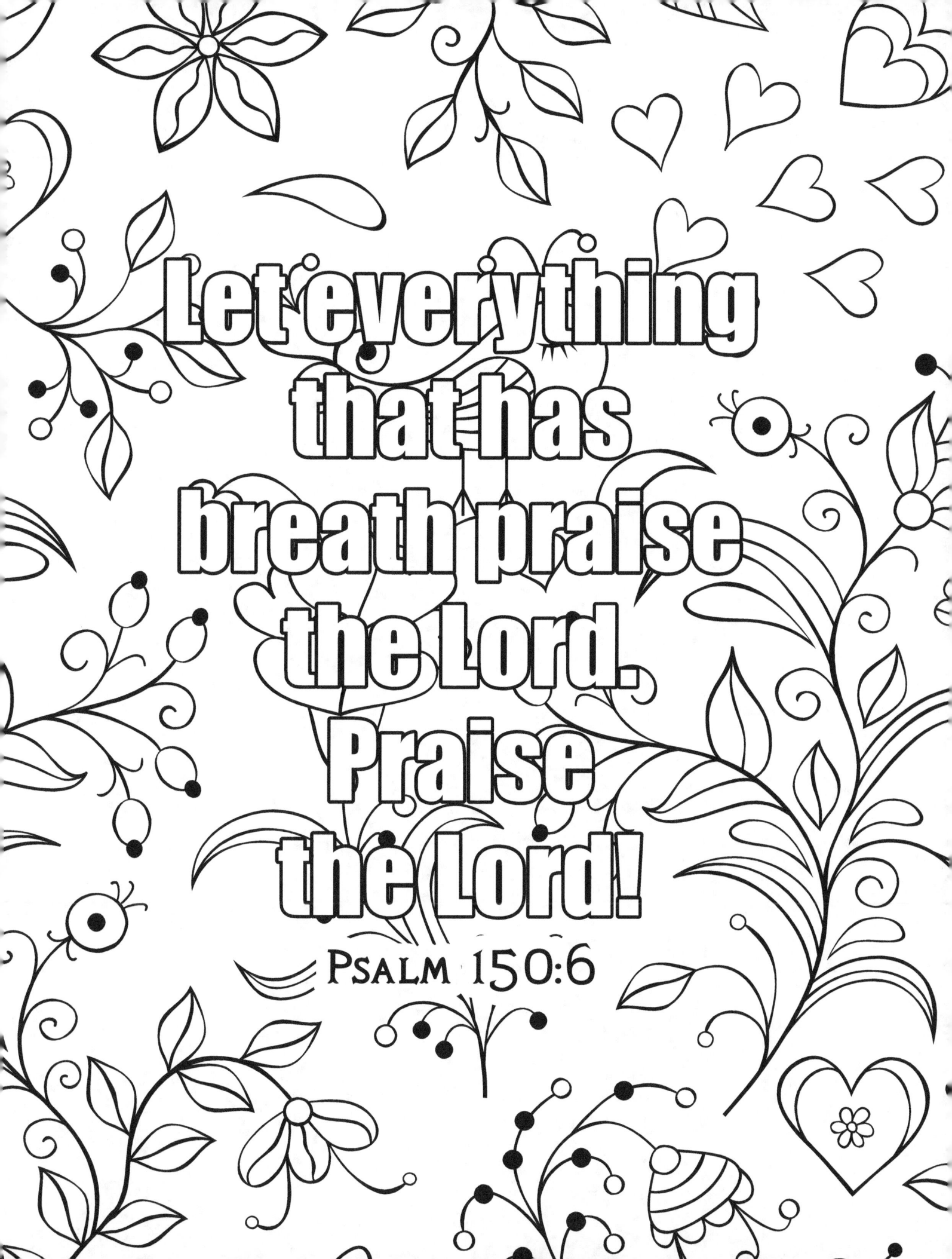